LOST MANORS

A history of the townships and
alehouses of Gateacre and Childwall

Best wishes

[signature]

STUART
RIMMER

Paperback ISBN-13: 978-1-8384144-0-5
.ePub eBook ISBN-13: 978-1-8384144-1-2
.Mobi eBook ISBN-13: 978-1-8384144-2-9

The author would like to thank the following – Conservation Team Leader Annie Starkey and the staff at Liverpool Archives, the staff at Lancashire Archives and the Cheshire Archives, Stephen Lloyd at Knowsley Hall Estate Office, Lorna Hyland and Charlotte Murray at the Merseyside Maritime Museum Archives, the Gateacre Society, Alan David Wilson, Janis Winkworth, Linda Sealey

Special thanks to Mike Chitty of the Gateacre Society for his diligent scrutiny and erudite critique.

CONTENTS

INTRODUCTION

In 2018 I wrote a book entitled 'The Old Inns, Taverns and Beer Houses of Woolton', in which I endeavoured to uncover the lost and forgotten licensed houses of Woolton Village and its immediate vicinity. As I conducted my research I concentrated upon what is considered modern-day Woolton, to the exclusion of the pubs of nearby Gateacre. Given how closely the two villages have always been linked, this was something I was to later regret.

In order to redress this, I embarked upon a period of research and writing with the intention of focussing upon Gateacre and the old Little Woolton Township. As I began to delve into the origins and stories of the surviving pubs like the Black Bull, Bear and Staff and Brown Cow, and those which have disappeared relatively recently, such as the Railway Inn, Halfway House and Bridge Inn, I began to unearth information about a far older period in the area's history. I found myself reaching back into records which were over 400 years old, and which revealed details of a landscape, community, and a number of ancient alehouses, that have disappeared into the mists of time leaving little trace. It was a landscape which belonged to another era, before the housing estates and modern roads arrived, before Gateacre had formed into a village and when Netherley and Belle Vale were the names of mansion houses rather than the suburbs they are today. Details of long forgotten licensed houses such as The Dog, Rosamund Finch's House, Skillington House, and inn keepers such as William Tarleton, Henry Halewood and James Welling, began to reveal themselves to me from the dimness of the past. Fascinated, I resolved to find out all I could about them and where the old alehouses might have stood, and my project took on a new dimension.

As well as information about the old inns and alehouses of Little Woolton, I uncovered facts and details about other aspects of the ancient township's history which are just as interesting and little known. I decided to broaden the scope of this book to include some of the details of that forgotten era, as not only do I believe it will be of interest to those with a penchant for local history, but it gives the narratives of the old licensed houses some context. I felt compelled to provide brief overviews of the histories of Gateacre and Little Woolton, as well as short histories of the Brettargh Holt, the Lee, and the Grange. The ancient sources offered a new perspective, one which I hope will enlighten even the keenest local historians, and although key events in English History, such as the Reformation, the Civil War and the restoration of the monarchy, are well known, it is interesting to see them played out at a local level.

As I carried out my work, it became clear to me that Little Woolton has, over the centuries, had strong links to the bordering township of Childwall, and their histories are intertwined. They shared a parish church, manor court, market, and had common landowners and manorial lords and ladies. Not wishing to make the same mistake as I did when writing my previous book, I made a decision to encompass Childwall within this work. I have therefore included a brief history of Childwall, containing some little known and perhaps forgotten aspects of it, along with the stories of the Childwall Abbey, and the two long-lost inns of the village.

As this work encompasses the period from Tudor times to the early 20th century, I have also given an overview of the history of Gateacre's Georgian brewery, as well as other tales from Victorian and Edwardian times. These include an account of Gateacre's infamous and deadly 'Red Hill' and the Gateacre shooting incident from 1895, which caused a stir at the time. These stories serve to provide an insight into the social history of the area.

Having provided a summary of what is to be found in the pages that follow, I feel just as obliged to point out what is not included. I have not written about the area's 20th century pubs, which sprang up to cater for the residents of the new housing estates which began to arrive in the 1930s. These more modern pubs included the Coronation, Cat's Whiskers, Falstaff, Highwayman and Turtle, though ironically they are all now gone. While they deserve an honourable mention, their origins, existence and demise are all more or less within living memory. Readers of this book may have frequented them and known them well, and nothing I could produce from third hand research would compare with the actual memories and experiences of those who were acquainted with them. Likewise, the relatively modern Childwall Fiveways is not included here. The remit of this book was always intended to be the older pubs whose existence or origins lie further in the past, and which are perhaps in danger of being forgotten. Another local pub not covered in this book is the Halfway House on Woolton Road. While this old former beer house sits within the boundary of modern day Childwall, it started life within the old township of Wavertree. A history of this old public house would undoubtedly be interesting and useful, but Wavertree is a whole other area of research. Perhaps it is one for future consideration.

Mention must also be made of the Gateacre Hall Hotel, which stood in the Nook off Halewood Road. The Nook was a residential or 'occupation' road dating back to the 17th century or earlier, allowing access to a cluster of dwellings. One of those dwellings, the house of John Williamson, built in 1652, became part of Gateacre Hall, which was converted into the Hotel in 1964. Sadly, this building is now also demolished, replaced with modern apartment blocks. The developers of the site have at least preserved part of the ancient building that once stood there in the form of a stone door surround, the date of the building carved into its lintel, which is displayed in the car park as a monument to a lost era.

Finally, I make no apology for the occasional rollcall of dates and names. Although at times they appear as little more than lists , the information is hard won through hours of research, and any true effort at producing a comprehensive historical account would be incomplete without them. That being said, where I am able, I have attempted to flesh out the cold facts with those tales and reports from the time that have come to light. Of course, the vast majority of occurrences over the past 450 years, as fascinating as we would undoubtedly find them, were not recorded, regardless of how much I wish they had been. But, what I hope I have achieved is a fresh, and at times enlightening, account of the history of two once rural townships that are now lost to the sprawling urbanisation that came with the expansion of the city of Liverpool.

THE TOWNSHIP OF LITTLE WOOLTON

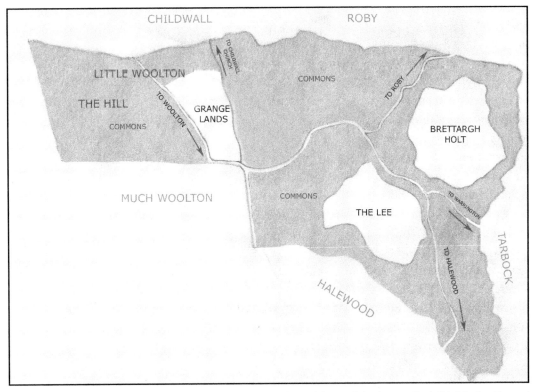

(Fig.1) Map showing the locations of the original ancient commons, thoroughfares and the three smaller 'vills' of the Lee, Brettargh Holt and Little Woolton which merged to form the larger township or manor of Little Woolton.

The township or manor[1] of Little Woolton encompassed modern-day Gateacre, Belle Vale and Netherley, an area which was, even up to the mid-20th century, mostly rural. New housing estates, roads and thoroughfares arrived as the 20th century progressed, rendering the landscape almost unrecognisable compared to how it had been over the previous centuries. Ancient roads and highways[2] which ran through the township have been erased and built over, and new, larger roads now cut across the crofts, meadows, heys and closes that made up the old farms and estates. As well as the roads, many of the brooks and streams that coursed through the township are gone. Much of Childwall Brook and its many tributaries have long since dried up, been filled in or culverted, rendering the old stone bridges, such as Naylor's Bridge and the Bean Bridge[3], redundant. If a person who lives today was to be transported back to the early 1600s they would see little that is familiar, except perhaps the rise of Gateacre Brow leading towards the undeveloped common land of the hill, or the sweep of the Belle Vale Road as it curved out towards the Holt lands, though both roads would be just narrow tracks made up of sand and stones.

The sprawling township that Little Woolton became did not start out as one large area, but rather three separate distinct areas or 'vills'. These were the Brettargh or Brettargh Holt, the Lee and the original Little Woolton, which consisted of the Grange and the hill. Prior to the early 17th century, the estates were separated by areas of common or waste land upon which the roads and highways had formed. This land was eventually enclosed and rented out to local tenants, leaving the highways to mark the borders of the former vills. From around 1630 onwards, the only remaining common land of any magnitude was on Woolton Hill, west of the highway from Woolton to Liverpool (modern day Woolton Road), along with one or two small, unenclosed patches dotted about the township.

The documented history of both Much Woolton and Little Woolton, can be traced back to the 12th century and earlier. In 1189, John, Baron of Halton, granted lands in Much and Little Woolton to the religious order of the Knights Hospitallers of St John of Jerusalem. The order originated as a group of monks who kept a house in Jerusalem for the reception of pilgrims who, having reached the city after long journeys, were in need of food and shelter. Due to illness or injuries they had suffered on their often arduous travels, they at times required nursing, and the monks did their best to tend to their ailments. Their house therefore became a place of both lodging and healing, from which the word 'hospital' is derived. There came a point in time when those making such pilgrimages increasingly found themselves under physical threat and in need of protection, but the monks, being forbidden carry weapons, could not provide it for them. They petitioned the Pope, asking permission to bear arms, and their request was granted. Thus the monks became knights, as well as priests and nurses, and the order of the Knights Hospitallers was born. The warrior priests gained great respect and won the support of the wealthiest noble families in England, who often made contributions to the order with gifts of land. So it was that in 1189 the Knights were given lands within the townships of Much and Little Woolton, albeit they were to lose the land in Little Woolton to the monks of Stanlow Abbey in 1204 and did not regain it until 1292. Incidentally, the land occupied by the monks during their time in the area was known as the Grange, and roughly corresponds with modern day Gateacre. The legacy of the monks of Stanlow persists today, if only in the names of Grange Lane, Grange Lodge, the Lower Grange and Gateacre Grange.

Upon regaining the Grange Lands in 1292, the Knights of St John also added the lands of the Brettargh to their holdings. In 1338 a survey was conducted which took stock of the property held by the Knights in Woolton. Their assets consisted of a substantial house in Much Woolton with 50 acres[4] of arable land and 5 acres of meadow, as well as other lands which were rented out for a total of £8 per year. This house is believed to have stood where Woolton Hall was later built. The order also had lands in Little Woolton, and a water mill which stood on Childwall Brook. The brook had been dammed between what later became Naylor's Bridge and Netherley Bridge. Although the mill and dam are long gone, traces of their existence could still be found into the 19th century in the names of certain features in the locality. There were several tracts of land near to Naylor's Bridge called the Dam Meadows and Dam Crofts, and an old house called Peck Mill House, which stood on the original Wood Lane, is believed to have been named for its association with the mill. The Hospitallers held the lands in Much and Little Woolton for several centuries and after such humble beginnings had become very wealthy.

The reformation of King Henry VIII saw the end of the ownership of Woolton by the Knights Hospitallers. In the 1530s the land was seized by the crown, and the manor of Little Woolton was granted to William Norris of Speke, whose name appears on the surviving manorial records from 1547. By this time, the three vills of Holt, Lee and Grange had coalesced to form a single township. Little Woolton, or 'Woolton Parva' to give it its Latin name (Much Woolton being 'Woolton Magna'), having originally just consisted of the Grange lands, had grown to encompass a greater area than the now incongruously named Much Woolton.

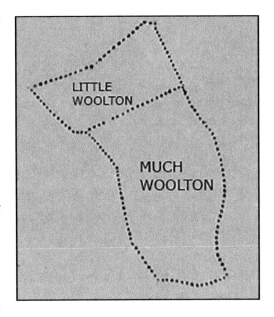

(Fig.2) A conjectural plan showing the original proportions of Much and Little Woolton when first named as such in the earliest period after their formation. The Grange estate would later expand east, and the incorporation of the separate vills of the Lee and the Brettargh Holt into Little Woolton in the late middle ages, would have the effect of making it the larger township in terms of area.

During the reign of Queen Mary, the Knights Hospitallers made a brief resurgence and tried to stake a claim on their former lands. However, in May 1559, following the reassertion by Elizabeth I of the English monarchy as head of the church in England, the era of the Knights was ended for good. Little Woolton began to settle into a more recognisable manorial system, with Norris at its head, and other wealthy families acquiring substantial estates of land. Initially the Grange was held by the Earl of Derby, while the Orme family acquired the Lee estate and the Brettargh family owned the Holt estate. With the permission of the Lord of the Manor, the common land between the three estates were gradually enclosed by the owners of the Lee, Holt and Grange. Pieces of this land were also leased and sold copyhold or freehold to other wealthy individuals. Due possibly to its fragmented origins, the Manor of Little Woolton boasted two manor houses, one situated at the Lee and the other at the Holt.

Notes:

[1]The terms 'township' and 'manor' can be seen to be more or less interchangeable, certainly as regards Little Woolton, Childwall, and Much Woolton and the territory they covered. Both terms are used in the ancient rolls of the manor court though in slightly different contexts. 'Within this township' usually relates to the activities and movement of the inhabitants, and 'within this manor' is more associated with the transfer and ownership of land. The boundaries of the manors and townships of Little Woolton and Childwall are analogous with each other, except, it seems, for a period in the first part of the 17th century when part of the manor of Childwall was described as lying just over the border in Little Woolton Township. This is probably due to the fact that the land in question (the Grange Field) was tenanted by individuals from Little Woolton, so, in the absence of a Childwall manorial court, it likely made sense for it to be administered by Little Woolton's officials. In terms of ownership it mattered little, as both manors were owned by the Earl of Derby in any event. Later, the

boundaries were modified so manor and township fell into accord.

[2]The original Wood Lane, Netherley Lane, Wambo Lane, Holt Lane and the old Lee Lane are all roads which have been erased by modern development.

[3]The 'Bean Bridge' was a bridge on what is now Belle Vale Road over a tributary of Childwall Brook, near to modern day King's Drive (see fig.28). In ancient township records it is also referred to as the Beny Bridge, and the Bene Bridge. There was also a parcel of land nearby known as the Bean Bridge Meadow. The name itself most likely derives from *Beinn*, which is Old Norse for straight, inferring that the bridge was a straight bridge, possibly level with the road surface rather than arching over the stream it crossed. This cannot be ascertained for certain, as no pictures appear to exist of the ancient bridge, which is long gone.

[4]It should be borne in mind that the 'acre' referred to in the periods before the 19th century were acres of *large* measure, also known as Cheshire or Lancashire acres, and were over twice the size of the standardised or statute acres of the modern era.

THE LEE

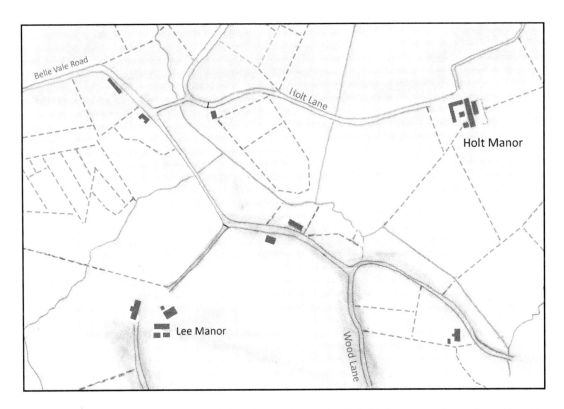

(Fig.3) Map showing the locations of the Lee and the Holt manor houses when Little Woolton was a still a mostly rural township. Both buildings are now demolished, with a golf clubhouse on the site of the Lee, while the site of the Holt is currently unbuilt upon. The broken lines represent the fences, hedges, walls or ditches which would have formed the boundaries of different plots of land.

The Lee is one of Little Woolton's ancient homesteads, and appears in the Domesday Book of 1086 as Wibaldeslei. Referred to in some historic sources as Ulbert's Land, and also Wibald's or Wigbald's Lee, it consisted of the area between modern day Belle Vale Road, and the border with Halewood.

Along with the other estates, the Lee became part of the larger Little Woolton Manor following the reformation and one of the earliest recorded occupants of the Lee in this era is George Orme, who appears in the court rolls of William Norris in 1549 as 'Georgius Orme de Lee'. Several other Ormes appear in the rolls but are not given the 'de Lee' appellation. The Lee estate had its manor house, or capital messuage, which stood in the centre of the estate[1]. Orme owned the house freehold, but paid the Lord of the Manor a ground rent of 'two barbed arrows'. This rent became a tradition, and was still paid by the owners of the Lee until as late as the 19th century.

By 1557, George Orme had died, and Thomas Orme is shown as 'of the Lee', with Alice

Orme recorded as George Orme's widow. In the court rolls of 1558, the transfer of the late George Orme's lands to Thomas Orme is recorded, Thomas being described as '*filius*', or his son. The new owner of the Lee went on to be a prominent and active member of the local manor court.

In 1582, Thomas Orme died and was buried at Childwall Church. At the time of his death the Lee estate consisted of the manor house, and 19 acres of grounds, upon which stood some smaller cottages which were let to tenants. As well as the lands immediately attached to the house, the owners of the Lee also rented much of the adjacent land and properties from the Lord of the Manor on a copyhold basis. The estate passed to Orme's son, also called Thomas, and who is referred to in the court rolls as Thomas Ormeson, perhaps in deference to the family's Scandinavian heritage. Over the years that followed in the late 16th and early 17th centuries, Thomas Orme junior added other parcels of land to the estate, and the family's holdings grew.

Thomas Orme was the last of the family to own the Lee, and when he died in 1623, his estate consisted of the manor house, 31 acres of freehold land and 33 acres of copyhold land which for he paid 12 shillings and 11 pence rent to the lord of the manor. In 1624, with Orme having no heir of inheritance age[2], the estate came into the possession of Thomas Ireland from Bewsey, and remained with the Ireland family for several generations.

In June 1626 a curious series of events took place at the Lee, when owner Thomas Ireland made a complaint to the local Justices of the Peace, Richard Bold and George Ireland (who may or may not have been a direct relation). Ireland complained that Edward Fayrehurst, a yeoman from Liverpool, and his wife Jane, along with Edward Fryer and his wife Elizabeth, also from Liverpool, had '*with force and strong hand*' entered the Lee manor house and were '*keeping and houlding the house with force of arms*'. What had prompted such an action is unclear. Perhaps Fayrehurst and Fryer were in dispute with Ireland and believed that they had a right to take over the house. What is clear is that Thomas Ireland was not residing at the Lee, and the invasion of the house had taken place without his knowledge. Ireland had turned to the two Justices and requested that they remedy the situation. Richard Bolton and George Ireland duly attended the Lee and found Fayrehurst, Fryer and their wives at the house. Deeming their actions unlawful, contrary to a statute '*made and provided in the fifteenth yeare of Kinge Richard the Second*', the Justices had them arrested and conveyed to Lancaster gaol. There they were to be held until they paid a fine, which was assessed to be 25 shillings for each of them, after which they were set free.

When Thomas Ireland died in 1639, the Lee estate was left to his daughter Margaret. By 1647, the Lee was in the possession of Margaret Ireland's cousin Gilbert Ireland whom she had married. Gilbert Ireland also owned land and houses elsewhere, most notably the 'Hutt' in Halewood where he and his wife resided. Although the Lee was owned by the Ireland family, no Ireland appears to have ever lived there. In fact, following the departure of the Ormes, the ownership and occupancy of the Lee was a complicated affair. The estate was held and occupied by a series of owners, lease holders and tenants. In 1639 when Thomas Ireland died, Thomas Johnson was the occupant of Lee Hall, with much of the surrounding land and houses let to other tenants. Later Johnson's son, William, was tenant and in the 1650s the lease was acquired by Edward Aspinall, and after his death was held by his widow Ellinor. In 1671 the occupant of the Lee was William Barker, an under tenant to Aspinall.

Gilbert Ireland died in 1675, and after his death Margaret Ireland surrendered ownership of the Lee estate to Thomas Cooke of Bewsey. Margaret died not long after, but Cooke held the Lee estate until 1679, when he surrendered it into the possession of Richard Atherton. Atherton was a cousin of Margaret Ireland. Again, it appears that neither Cooke nor Atherton lived at the Lee, and the lease was still in the hands of Ellinor Aspinall. Widow Aspinall was to remarry cleric Thomas Crompton, and the lease duly passed to him. The Cromptons continued to let out the Lee to under tenants. In 1699 Thomas Crompton, by this time a widower, died and his lease appeared to die with him. In 1700 the occupant of the Lee is shown as William Claughton.

In 1706 owner Richard Atherton died, however his son and heir, John, was still an infant and too young to inherit the estate. The estate lay in trust until 1724, when John Atherton reached the age of 23 and was old enough to take ownership of the house and lands. At the time the Lee was occupied by Richard Legh esq. and in 1726 Atherton sold the lease for the Lee to Thomas Brettargh of Manchester, son of James Brettargh of the Holt. However, the Brettargh family were on the decline, and by 1732 Thomas Brettargh was bankrupt, forfeiting the Lee estate accordingly. For the next few years, ownership of the Lee and its various parcels of land, houses and cottages was in some disarray, though Richard Legh remained occupant of Lee Hall manor house throughout this period.

In 1736 the Lee estate was acquired jointly by John Okill, a merchant from Liverpool, and Samuel Leigh who was a gentleman from Thelwall. By 1747 Okill was sole owner of Lee Hall and the attached estate, and the Lee was to remain in the hands of the Okill family for over a century. Unlike all previous owners since the Ormes, John Okill actually took up residency of the Lee. Okill also set about consolidating his assets, and took the opportunity to purchase lands previously only rented from the lord of the manor by his predecessors. In 1771, having lived at the Lee for several decades, Okill began to rebuild the centuries old Lee Hall. John Okill died in 1773, before his new house had been completed. The estate was inherited by his nephew James Okill who, before long, was able to complete the building that had been started by his uncle. The original house of the Lee had now been replaced with a grand Georgian mansion house, for which Okill still paid the traditional ground rent of two barbed arrows to the Lord of the Manor. James Okill lived in the new house for over 40 years, until he died in 1815. The house and estate was inherited by his son John Okill, who himself lived at the Lee for over three decades.

An interesting incident occurred at Lee Hall in 1850, when, on 5th October that year, a small bore hole, or 'gimlet' hole, was discovered in the front door of the house. This aroused suspicions that someone was planning to commit a burglary at the house, and so John Okill hired three men – John Godard, William Nichols and Richard Kelly – to lie in wait at the house in anticipation of an encroachment. Sure enough, at 2am on the morning of the 7th October, Godard was on watch inside the entrance way of the house when he heard a grating sound at the door. He woke the other two men and they waited for a while inside the property expecting an entry to be made. When the incursion was not forthcoming they armed themselves with what they later described as 'defensive' weapons and made their way via the rear of the premises to the front of the house. There they found two men busy boring a hole in the front door panel with an instrument. A scuffle ensued, and one man was captured while the other made good his escape leaving his coat in the hands of one of the hired guards.

Two gimlets and a hat were found nearby. The captured man was handed over to the Woolton police and secured at the bridewell on Woolton Street. However, during the night, the man forced the bars of his cell and escaped custody never to be seen again. Several days later, Woolton's police inspector, John MacDonald, received some information as to the identity of the male who had originally fled the scene of the attempted burglary of Lee Hall, and a man called William Wilson was apprehended. Wilson appeared before the magistrates at the Woolton Mechanics Institute on 21st October where he pleaded not guilty. Wilson, described as 'a respectable looking man' was a convicted felon and was well known to the police. The three witnesses appeared before the magistrates, but were unable to satisfy the bench that Wilson was the man who tried to break into Okill's house and he was released.

John Okill never married and died in October 1851 intestate and having no direct heir. The Lee Estate was acquired by Thomas Dutton, and his brother William, sons of John Okill's cousin. Due to the lack of a will, the Duttons struggled for many years to prove their title to the estate, despite them taking occupancy relatively soon after Okill's death. The Duttons had not been at Lee Hall long when they were themselves involved in an incident of some drama. In the early hours of Friday morning, 12th March 1852, a constable from the Woolton police was on duty in Gateacre when he saw flames lighting up the night sky from the direction of Lee Hall. Making to the scene he saw that several hay stacks were ablaze, and the Duttons were alerted from their respective slumbers. A messenger on horseback was duly despatched to inform the fire brigade in Liverpool. The messenger reached Liverpool at 4.30am, and by 5am two horse drawn engines and a compliment of men, led by fire officer Hewitt, were at the scene. They were soon joined by an engine from the West of England Insurance Company, under the supervision of Superintendent Barrett. They found four large haystacks on fire and, using water from a nearby fishpond, set about dousing the flames. After about an hour, the fire had been extinguished, but not before about 60 tons of hay had been destroyed. The conclusion reached by the police and fire officers at scene was that the fire had been started deliberately. A £100 reward was offered to anyone who could provide information as to the perpetrators, but no one was ever caught.

The Duttons did not reside at the Hall itself, rather Thomas Dutton and his family lived at Garden Lodge nearby and rented the Hall itself out to Liverpool brass founder and politician John Hays Wilson[3]. In December 1862, Wilson found himself in dispute with over 50 residents of Much and Little Woolton which resulted in him issuing summonses against them. It appears that the persons in question lived on or near the Nook estate off Halewood Road, which bordered with the grounds of the Lee. These residents were making use of an 'open sewer' for their waste and effluence, which Wilson claimed was a hazardous and offensive nuisance. The case was to be heard at the Wavertree petty sessions, but before the proceedings commenced the legal representatives of both sides agreed to find a solution out of court, as the Woolton residents could little afford the cost of expensive litigation. The case was adjourned to allow the Little Woolton Board of Guardians and the Much Woolton Nuisance Removal Committee to come together and work out a solution to the problem. This they were subsequently able to do to the satisfaction of Wilson and all parties concerned.

(Fig.4) The Georgian Lee Hall built by John Okill on the site if the earlier manor house of the Ormes and the Irelands. Pictured in 1955, empty and awaiting demolition. Picture courtesy of Liverpool Record Office, Liverpool Libraries.

John Hays Wilson died in May 1881, and with Lee Hall now empty, an effort was made to sell the estate. The Lee was purchased by John Scales for £75,000, but shortly afterwards Scales found himself bankrupt, and had to forfeit the property. In 1882, the estate, then consisting of 250 acres, was purchased by a company which had been set up solely to buy and develop the extensive lands of the Lee. The estate, which included not only the Hall, but a mansion house on Belle Vale Road called Throstle Nest, another near the church called Lee Vale, the Bridge Inn, Netherley House, and numerous other houses and cottages, was acquired for £95,000. The company, called the 'Lee Hall Land Company Ltd.' then sought to raise money by offering shares, with a promise of profits and returns through future development of the estate. Before long, Lee Hall became Lee Hall Farm, its fate much like that of Little Woolton's other former Manor House, the Holt.

A house as old as the Lee did not come without stories of ghosts and hauntings, and no one loved a ghost story more than the Victorians. This era spawned two ghostly legends which started amongst the local inhabitants and persisted for many years. The first, which is supposed to have occurred at an unspecified date, is that an ancestor of the Duke of Wellington married one of the daughters of the wealthy family who were living at the hall, and soon after the marriage was found to be having an affair with another woman. The wife's enraged parents captured the errant husband and hanged him from gallows by the lodge gates, where his body was left to be devoured by rats. Thereafter, it was said that on certain nights the sound of a rope creaking in the wind could be heard, and anyone who heard it met with misfortune.

The other story was that a man and his wife, also unnamed, once lived at the hall. A period of several weeks passed by during which they had not been seen, and concerned locals decided to investigate. Upon approaching the house, they found the woman stabbed to death in a dark passageway, and the man a raving lunatic. The screams of the dead woman and the cries of her insane husband could sometimes be heard in the still of the night.

Such was the persistence of these stories that, in 1938, a local newspaper organised a ghost hunt at Lee Hall, much to the annoyance of the then resident Horace Jones. Jones denied all rumours of hauntings, and stated that in the 35 years he had been at Lee Hall he had heard and seen nothing, but would like to get his hands on the people who started the rumours! In a final rejoinder he stated that he had not so much been troubled by ghosts as by people ringing him up to enquire about ghosts, or trespassing on his land looking for them, and that he would be glad when the house was demolished, as was planned at that time.

Much of the land that made up the Lee estate was eventually acquired by the Liverpool Corporation. The proposed Kings Drive dual carriageway, which was to be a major route through the area, entered a hiatus at the onset of the Second World War from which it never recovered. Following the war, the Corporation began to build the housing estates that stand on the former Lee land along Belle Vale Road. Having stood empty for many years, the Lee Hall manor house was considered in too dilapidated a state to save and was finally demolished in 1956. The last tenant of Lee Hall, Horace Jones, has been immortalised by the Corporation's engineers and town planners. Just off Belle Vale Road is a small road leading onto the modern estate called Jones Farm Road.

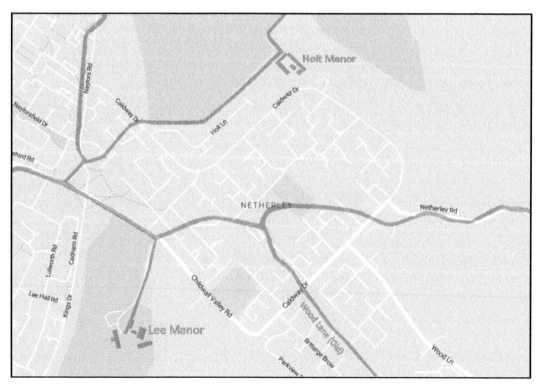

(Fig.5) Overlay onto a modern map showing the original routes of the old roads (dark grey) through what is now Netherley, and the locations of the Holt and Lee manor houses.

Notes:

[1]The original manor house would have stood approximately where the club house for the Lee Park Golf Club now stands. The course was formed in the 20th century on land that was formerly part of the Lee estate.

[2]Other entries in the court rolls show the age at which a son or daughter was allowed to inherit their parents' estate at that time was considered to be 23 years.

[3]Perhaps Wilson's most enduring achievement was as Chairman of the Liverpool Water Committee in the 1870s, when he was instrumental in the success of the Vyrnwy Water Scheme which modernised and improved the supply of water to the city. He was highly regarded and well-respected, and in 1883 the ornate stone shelter and drinking fountain, which is a prominent feature of the green at the centre of Gateacre Village, was erected in his memory and bears his name.

THE HOLT

(Fig.6) Stones salvaged from the ruins of the demolished Holt manor house bearing the initials of William Brettargh, the Brettargh coat of arms and part of the 16th century date stone. Had they not been salvaged, these stones would likely have been disposed of and lost forever. Thankfully they were saved from such a fate and have been incorporated into the garage of a house on Grange Lane.

Although the Lee was the primary manor house for the manor in the mid-16th century, it was eventually superseded in importance and status by the Holt. The Holt was another of the original three main estates of Little Woolton, and was originally called the Brettargh or the Brettargh Holt. It has long been associated with the Brettargh family, who originally took their name from their association with it. The estate was situated in the area of modern day Netherley, and a misspelled reference to the Brettargh can be found in the name of one of the modern roads in that area called Brittarge Brow.

The word or name of Brettargh – originally pronounced as 'Bretter' - has had associations with the area since at least 1185, when the lands or 'vill' of the Brettargh are mentioned in early deeds and charters for the area. There is evidence that in 1204, when the lands of Little Woolton were taken from the Knights Hospitallers and granted to the Abbey of Stanlow, that Little Woolton and the Brettargh were separate entities and divided by an area of common or waste land. By the end of the 13th century however, when the Knights of St John recovered ownership of Little Woolton, they also claimed the Brettargh, and the occupant of the land at the time had to pay rent to the Hospitallers. Eventually the two estates merged and, along with the Lee, would come to form the larger township of Little Woolton.

In about 1324, the Brettargh came into the occupancy of Avice de Huyton, and her husband Roger the Walker[1], and together they took the name 'de Brettargh' or 'of the Brettargh'. The Brettargh Holt remained in the hands of the descendants of Roger and Avice for nearly five centuries, and it seems that for several generations the forename William was the traditional name for the eldest son and heir of the estate. In 1399, William de Brettargh the elder and William de Brettargh the younger held the estate which consisted of a messuage and 120 acres. In 1527, William de Brettargh died in possession of a cottage, dovecote and 100 acres of land in Little Woolton, for which he had paid 18 pence rent to the Knights Hospitallers. In 1569, following the suppression and disbanding of the Knights Hospitallers, the court rolls of William Norris show a William de Brettargh as occupying the Holt estate and paying rent to the Norris family.

Before long, the 'de' was dropped from the name, and the family became just Brettargh. In 1583, William Brettargh bought a part of the Holt estate outright as a freehold from Norris, and he built the grand Brettargh Holt manor house. Alongside the Lee, this became Little Woolton's second capital messuage. The Holt increased in importance, and the estate increased in size as more parcels of land and properties were added to it. Brettargh, who died in 1585, also owned land in Much Woolton, the Aigburth manor house and estate, and lands in Garston.

Upon the death of William Brettargh, the estate was inherited by his grandson, also called William. Young William Brettargh was only 24 years old when he acquired the Holt, though he was already considered a prominent Childwall parishioner with a great deal of influence. In 1600 he was appointed as High Constable of the West Derby Hundred, and as a staunch puritan and protestant conformist, was often at the vanguard of the hunt for, and prosecution of, catholic recusants within the Childwall parish. This brought about a rivalry with Edward Norris of Speke, a renowned recusant who was believed to harbour priests at Speke Hall, his place of abode. It is thought that after Brettargh's marriage to his second wife Ann in 1601, his puritanical leanings mellowed somewhat, as did his enmity towards Norris. After their death, William and Ann Brettargh's son, Nehemiah, was next to inherit the Holt.

Nehemiah Brettargh became the owner of the Holt in 1628, following the death of his widowed mother. A Royalist with a military background, he did not display the puritanical religious leanings of his father. In 1644, during the Civil War, he held the rank of lieutenant and was involved in the successful defence of Lathom House, the seat of James Stanley, Earl of Derby, when it was besieged by parliamentary forces led by Sir Thomas Fairfax. Also unlike his father, Nehemiah Brettargh did not live at the Holt, rather it was occupied by Edward Stockley, who had married Brettargh's daughter. Stockley was the steward of the Little Woolton Manor Court, which was held at the Holt in this period. When Nehemiah's son, James Brettargh, came of age in 1653, he also took up residency of the Holt, essentially becoming the master of the house. Nehemiah Brettargh was, for most of his life, known as a heavy drinker. In 1659, having gone to bed 'merry', he died in his sleep.

James Brettargh inherited his father's estate. Having come into the ownership of the Holt during the Cromwellian era, he had very shrewdly declared himself a staunch parliamentarian, and also gained a reputation as a particularly zealous and puritanical preacher. As a supporter of Parliament, James was able to protect his assets, however, it is reported that after the restoration of the monarchy in 1661, James Brettargh's 'mask fell off' and he became an excessive drinker like his father. In fact, it was to be his end, as, in 1665, whilst riding home from Warrington one night after a drinking session, he fell from his horse sustaining injuries from which he never recovered. He was buried in the chancel of Childwall Church.

The Holt passed to James' son, Jonathan Brettargh, and then down the Brettargh line, until the last of the Brettargh family to be associated with the estate was James Brettargh, who inherited it in 1747. James lived at the Holt Manor House, but finding himself in debt had gradually began to sell off parts of his holdings. By the time of his death in 1786, James Brettargh was insolvent. As such there was not a great deal for Brettargh to leave his heirs, and the remainder of his estate and house were sold to Thomas Dobb to cover the debts.

The days of the great Brettargh family in Little Woolton were over after almost half a millennium. The estate was offered for sale by auction in 1795 and was described as consisting of over 195 acres, with a good stream suitable for running a mill, and plenty of sources of marl. It was also claimed that coal may be found on some parts of the estate. The Holt came into the possession of several wealthy owners thereafter, most notably Thomas Rawson in 1799, and Francis Henry Froes in 1846. By this time it had ceased to be regarded as a manor house, and was instead occupied by a series of tenant farmers. By the late 19th century it was known as Holt Hall Farm, being occupied in the late 19th and early 20th centuries by farmer John Scotson and his son James.

It was during the tenure of James Scotson that a violent and tragic incident occurred in the grounds of the Holt. On 11th May 1917, a ploughman in the employ of Scotson came across the body of a woman in a field near to the lane leading from Naylor's Road to Holt Hall. A cord was tied tightly around her neck, knotted in two places, and a handkerchief stuffed into her mouth. The woman was identified as 26 year old Miriam Annie Napier from Huyton, the wife of a serving soldier called Ernest Leopold Napier. The next day, the body of Ernest Napier, who had been home on leave, was found in a lavatory in Bristol. He had died from poisoning. A note was found with the body which read, 'sorry for what I have done. I love my wife and cannot help taking this step. It's no good saying more. I am about to take my life.' An inquest was held into the death of Miriam Napier, during which a picture of a marriage blighted by episodes of violence by Napier towards his wife, infidelity and separation emerged. Members of the families of both deceased described an unhappy and turbulent marriage which had been tempered somewhat by Napier's joining the army and being away from home. However, the situation had culminated in Ernest Napier taking his wife's life in a brutal manner while they were out for a walk in and around the Holt estate. At the inquest, Doctor Ernest Glynn gave evidence that the post mortem on Ernest had revealed he had been suffering from the first stages of pneumonia and might have been suffering from delusions. The jury returned a verdict that Napier had killed his wife while not being in his right mind.

Eventually, as the 20th century progressed, the Holt estate was sold off, most notably when Childwall Golf Club acquired much of the land for a new course in 1936, with lease for their previous site at Childwall Hall due to expire in 1938. It took the club three years to construct a new course and clubhouse at the Holt, and they moved to their new home on 6th June 1939. Thanks to its protected status as part of the Merseyside Green Belt, as well as the presence of the golf course, a large part of the once rural estate is still green, open and unbuilt upon. Other parts of the former Holt lands were acquired by the Liverpool Corporation and new housing estates were built in the 1960s which now form part of the modern day suburb of Netherley.

What had once remained of the old Holt manor house, and the subsequent farm buildings have been demolished. Remnants of the old 16th century house were saved from being lost forever when they were presented to the Gateacre Society in 1978 by Mrs Humphries, the last owner of Holt Hall Farm. They consist of a partial date stone, and the coat of arms and initials of William Brettargh. These stones can be found incorporated into the garage connected to Grange Lodge on Grange Lane in Gateacre (see fig.6). The site of the old Holt house sits in-between Childwall golf course and the modern Caldway Drive and is currently unbuilt upon.

(Fig.7) The site of the Brettargh Holt Manor House as it is now, sitting near the edge of Childwall Golf Course.

Notes:

[1]'Walker' is a surname derived from an occupation. In olden times, a walker, also referred to as a fuller, was a person who processed raw cloth, most commonly wool, for use in garment making etc. Therefore Roger the Walker is also recorded in some records as Roger the Fuller. The occupation died out during the industrial revolution, but the surnames Walker and Fuller still survive.

A BRIEF HISTORY OF
'THE GRANGE'

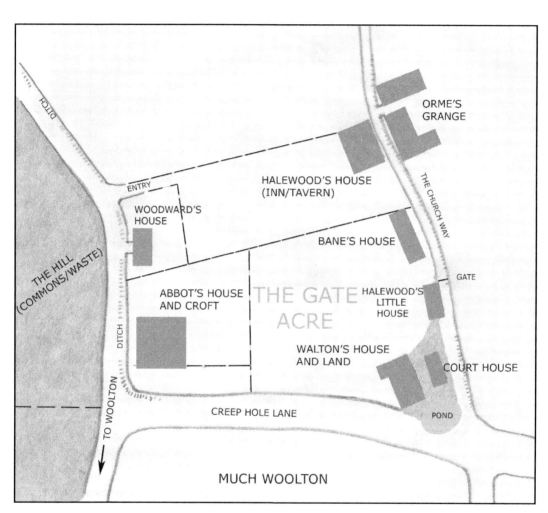

(Fig.8) The area around Gateacre Brow and Grange Lane in the mid to late 1600s (not to scale). Walton's House and the Court House would later become the Black Bull. Abbot's House would be replaced by the 'New Grange' in the 18th century. Bane's House is now known as Paradise Row. The gate shown across the Church Way, now Grange Lane, is that which gave the Gate Acre its name.

The estate known as the Grange, between modern day Grange Lane and Rose Brow, has been occupied since at least the 12th century. From 1189 Little Woolton was briefly in the possession of the Knights Hospitallers, until being re-granted to the Monks of Stanlow Abbey in 1204. The land occupied by the monks became known as the 'Grange', a grange in ancient times being the name given to agricultural land attached to or owned by a monastery. The monks, led by an Abbot, held two plough land and 100 acres of pasture, and established a messuage and mill. They also ran a school for catechumens, men who had not been baptised at birth and were seeking baptism into the Christian faith later in life. The estate stretched from the foot of Woolton Hill down to Grange Lane, and north towards the border with Childwall. Even after the monks had left the area, the estate retained the name of the Grange.

Following the reformation of the 1530s, when Little Woolton was seized by the crown, the Grange lands were purchased by the Earl of Derby. The Grange estate had expanded onto the commons east of Grange Lane, and a house was built on the newly enclosed land. The house, which was later referred to as the Old Grange or Lower Grange, stood on Grange Lane, and part of the old 16th Century structure still stands to this day. Amongst the earliest recorded tenants of the Grange estate are the Whitfield family, when in 1549 Thomas Whitfield was fined by the manor court for not maintaining his hedges. Over the ensuing years Thomas and William Whitfield are shown as occupants of the Grange house, which served as the principal house of the estate's owners over the centuries that followed. Eventually the Grange house and much of the surrounding estate was acquired by the Orme family, who continued to occupy it for over a century.

In 1629, William Earl of Derby leased a house and surrounding plot of land of about 8 acres, which was situated on the corner of modern day Gateacre Brow and Rose Brow, to Margaret Abbot. The house became known locally as Abbot's house, the grounds as Abbot's Croft, and the corner of Gateacre Brow and Rose Brow was known as Abbot's Corner. Gateacre Brow was known locally as 'Creep Hole Lane' in this period. At the bottom of the brow, on the site of what is now Gateacre Green, there was a pond of water known as the 'Creep Hole'. The house and grounds remained in the hands of the Margaret Abbot until she died in 1651. George Highfield acquired freehold ownership of the house and grounds, which he owned for nearly 30 years.

In 1680, William Davis acquired Abbot's House and Croft, as well as a house further along Rose Brow called Woodward's House, but in 1687 Davis died and the property was inherited by his widow Alice Davis.

In 1692 the old building was in a state of notable disrepair, which prompted the steward of the Little Woolton manorial court to order Alice Davis to repair the house or be fined. Davis was also responsible for maintaining the ditch between Abbot's Croft and the highway that became Rose Brow. This ditch had to be kept clear in order to take up the water which ran down from the common land of Woolton Hill. The hill was a notable source of running water which, if not dealt with, resulted in flooding of the road. As well as Davis, the other owners and tenants of land along Rose Brow and Woolton Road were responsible for the maintenance of the sections of the ditch which lay against their property. The manor court would repeatedly remind, or 'order', land owners to scour these ditches to keep them clear. At the court of 1693, Davis was found not to have repaired Abbot's House, and not to have maintained her ditch, and was fined a total of 50 shillings.

Alice Davis died in 1719, and Abbot's House was offered for sale. It is unclear who owned the house and land next, but in the mid-18th century, it was acquired by William Barrow who also bought the Grange estate and house on Grange Lane from the Orme family. He demolished Abbot's House and built a new house which he called the 'New Grange', and thereafter the original Grange on Grange Lane was referred to as the 'Old Grange'. After Barrow's death in 1791, the ownership of the Grange estate passed to his son Edward Barrow, and in 1794 he decided to sell the New Grange to Henry Fairclough. Barrow retained ownership of the Old Grange, which he rented to Joseph Turton.

Fairclough lived at the New Grange himself until his death in 1816, and the house and grounds fell into the hands of his executors. After a year in the occupation of Fairclough's widow, the premises were rented by William Duff, however the Grange was soon to have a new owner, and a new purpose.

In 1820 the New Grange, now referred to as the Higher Grange, was offered for sale. At the time it was described as comprising of eight acres of land, with an excellent walled garden stocked with fruit trees. There was also a flower garden, hot houses, two coach houses, a saddle house and two stables which could accommodate six horses. Here was also a small farm yard on the estate, with corn rooms and habitation for staff and labourers. The house itself consisted, on the ground floor, of a grand entrance hall, dining room, drawing and breakfast rooms, store rooms, butler's pantry, servant's hall, kitchen, and offices. The first floor had five bedrooms and a dressing room, and a further attic floor had another five bedrooms.

By 1821, the Higher Grange had been acquired by unmarried school mistress Sarah Lawrence who turned the building into a boarding school for girls. Lawrence ran the school herself for a number of years, before handing the running of the school to Sarah Ann Holland originally from Liverpool. In 1841 Holland is shown living there with her mother and two twin sisters Hannah and Helen, who are also teachers. At that time there were 28 pupils resident at the school ranging from 7 to 15 years of age. However, by 1851 the number of pupils had reduced to 13 and Holland was the sole teacher. By 1861 things seem to have picked up, and Holland had been joined by another two teachers with 20 pupils resident at the Grange. Holland ran the school at the Higher Grange until owner Sarah Lawrence decided to sell the property. Holland moved back to Liverpool to take up a similar position at a school in the city.

In 1862 Sarah Lawrence put the Higher Grange up for sale, and it was acquired by brewer Andrew Barclay Walker. Walker made many improvements to the property, enlarging and virtually rebuilding the Georgian house, and adding the high sandstone walls which still surround the house today. Upon Walker's death in 1893, the house and grounds came into the ownership and residency of his son, William Hall Walker.

William Hall Walker owned the Grange until 1917, when the house and estate was offered up for sale by auction. Walker moved away to Denbighshire, buying Horsley Hall in Gresford, and the association of the Walkers with Gateacre and the Grange came to an end.

Following the sale of the Grange, the house performed a number of functions. In the 1930s it was St Vincent's College School for Boys, and in 1940, the Grange was converted into the Virgo Potens charity hospital and convalescence home run by the Sisters of St Vincent's de Paul. It later also became a retired seafarers' residents, run by a Roman Catholic organisation called the Apostleship of the Sea. In modern times it has been converted into private apartments.

The legacy of the hill water that was an issue for Alice Davies and the later occupants of the Grange can still be seen to this day. When the walls on the opposite side of what is now Rose Brow and Woolton Road were constructed, a series of over 40 drainage holes were incorporated into the sandstone blocks to allow the water from the hill to drain onto the road and then into the grids that lead to the main Victorian sewer beneath Gateacre Brow. The holes were made near to the foot of the walls and run from the top of Gateacre Brow along to Woolton Road. Even after the widening of the road in the 20th century the drainage holes were retained, and are still present. The drainage holes also extend up Woolton Hill Road and can be seen in the walls on either side of the road. The subsequent building of the estates on Woolton Hill, and the accompanying drainage and sewerage systems means that very little hill water reaches the road today. Most of the holes are now dry and have become clogged or have even been cemented over, however a small amount of water from the ancient water source still occasionally flows from the four holes opposite Gateacre Brow.

(Fig.9) One of the 40 or so drainage holes in the sandstone walls along Rose Brow opposite the Grange. Intended to drain the water which from ancient times has run from the hill, only a few still occasionally emit water today, with most having dried up.

GRANGE LANE

At the time of the monks of Stanlow and the Knights Hospitallers, the road which is now called Grange Lane, also called Childwall Lane in the past, was a path to Childwall Church that skirted the edge of the Grange Lands. It would not have existed as a road in the form it appears today, but as an unnamed route or 'common path' taken by the inhabitants of Speke, Halewood and Much and Little Woolton as they made their way to church. As the Grange estate expanded to encompass the path in the 15th and 16th centuries, the route, known as the Churcheway, remained a right of way and access to it was tolerated by the owners of the land over which it now crossed. Despite this, it was not considered a public road but was under the control of the Lord of the Manor who required the various landowners to maintain it.

The upkeep of this important route to Childwall Church was enforced by the manorial court of Little Woolton. In the court rolls of 1555, several of the tenants, namely Richard Knoll, William Knoll, John Fletcher, Thomas Halewood, and Peter Walton, were given instructions by the manor court. They were ordered to gather together and perform maintenance on the 'Churcheway' which ran through their properties, from John Fletcher's house (which happened to be an alehouse) as far as the Cockshead[1] Brook. Over the years the various owners and residents of the land were periodically instructed to repair the thoroughfare when needed. In 1686, Ann Cockett was instructed to lay flags and make the way sufficiently passable where the road passed through her croft. In 1689, land owner Mordecai Cockett was ordered by the manorial court to make his section of the Churchway sufficiently passable to allow persons to traverse it. It appears he failed to do so to the satisfaction of the court and was fined 6 shillings and 8 pence. In 1709 Grange Lane was clearly described as a private road in the court rolls when John Berchall was fined a hefty 40 shillings for '*coming with his wagon past the Grange to and from Childwall it being no publick road and having eight horses*'. However, an entry in the records of Childwall Church in 1728 describes the Churchway as a 'public lane', though in light of all the evidence this is more likely to mean public right of way.

Eventually, the use of the Churchway became a nuisance to the landowners and tenants across whose land it ran, as they endured continual incursions onto their property, and the numerous gates across the lane being left open allowing cattle to stray. The number of obstructions along the way also made traversing the lane difficult for travellers to the church. This came to a head during the tenure as Lord of the Manor of Isaac Greene, and prompted the formation of Cuckoo Lane in 1748. Originally called 'New Lane', the road was built on Greene's own land and was paid for by Greene himself. Its purpose was to allow unrestricted access from the Woolton High Road (modern day Woolton Road/Rose Brow) near Gateacre Brow to the Churchway (Church Lane) in Childwall. Greene agreed with members of the parish that the new way would be kept open and free from gates and other obstructions. He also agreed that he, and his heirs after him, would pay for the ongoing maintenance of the new road. Whether this new road functioned as the alternative route to Childwall it was intended to be is open for debate, as it does not appear that Grange Lane ever really fell out of use.

Though it had long been a public right of way, Grange Lane continued to be considered a private road for many years. In 1843, in an advertisement for the sale of land in the area, it is described as a private road from Gateacre to Childwall. As late as the early 20th century there was still a gate at its far end, where the road now meets Gateacre Park Drive. In 1914, local historian Ronald Stewart-Brown describes Grange Lane as 'still at its north end a private road with gates across it'. It wasn't until 1955 that the road was declared public, and shortly after was widened and improved. Today, with the addition of 20th and 21st century housing along much of its length, it is a modern thoroughfare and residential road.

Notes.

[1]The origin of the name 'Cockshead' is interesting, and it can be traced back through the ancient records. The land at the end of Grange Lane which bordered with the township of Childwall, was owned for over a century by several generations of the Cockett family. A building erected on the land was a local landmark, and was referred to as Cockett's Hut or Cockett's Shed. Over time the names were shortened to Cockshut and Cocksshed or Cockshed, both terms referring to the same place. Over the years that followed the origin of the names became lost and forgotten, and they morphed into names that had more of a common sense meaning. Cockshut became Cockshoot before falling out of use, while Cockshed became Cockshead, which persisted long after the Cockett family had relinquished their lands and moved from the area. Even in the 19th and 20th centuries, the farm which sat on the land was called Cockshead Farm, though no one called Cockshead had ever owned it or lived there. Now, though the farm is gone and a housing estate has been built on the land, a vestige of the past remains, as two of the roads which have been built near the site of the old farm are called Cockshead Road and Cockshead Way.

GATEACRE VILLAGE

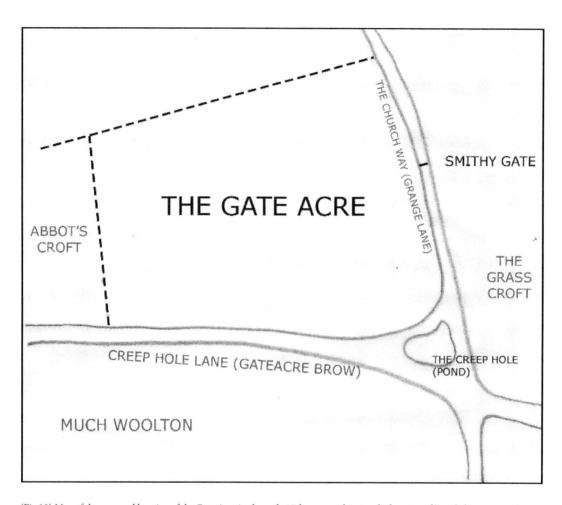

THE GATE ACRE

THE CHURCH WAY (GRANGE LANE)

SMITHY GATE

ABBOT'S CROFT

THE GRASS CROFT

CREEP HOLE LANE (GATEACRE BROW)

THE CREEP HOLE (POND)

MUCH WOOLTON

(Fig.10) Map of the proposed location of the Gate Acre in the early 17th century showing the location of 'Smithy' gate across Grange Lane after which the Gate Acre may have been named

The Village of Gateacre is less than a mile from Woolton Village, and the history of the two has always been inextricably linked. The small hub of the village, built around the crossroads at Gateacre Brow, Halewood Rd, Belle Vale Road, and Grange Lane – all relatively recent names – was once split between the two old townships of Much and Little Woolton. The south side of Gateacre Brow, on which sits the Bear and Staff inn and Brown Cow pub was in Much Woolton, a large township which also encompassed Woolton Village and part of modern-day Hunts Cross. The other side of Gateacre Brow, on which the Black Bull Inn is situated, was in Little Woolton. The fact that the village was so split can be explained by the fact that it emerged and developed after the township boundary had already been formed. There had been a monastic settlement on the Little Woolton side of the border since the 13th Century, and part of the monastic grange became known as the Gate Acre.

The origin of the name Gate Acre, which became Gateacre, has in the past been the subject of a certain amount of scrutiny and postulation. A prevailing theory has it that the name has a connection with an area of land in Much Woolton known as the Acrefield, which was situated in the vicinity of modern day Acrefield Road. The name Acrefield is recorded in a number of ancient charters from the 13th and 14th centuries, and is shown variously as the Aclaw Field, Akelou Field and Akelouysfeld. In time, the name settled into the more familiar sounding Acrefield. It is believed that Acrefield and its precursors derive from Ac-Lowe-Feld, meaning Oak Hill Field. This a well-reasoned argument, and in relation to the origin of Acrefield is compelling. By extension, the same reasoning has then been applied to Gateacre, the theory being that 'Gat' is Old Norse for way or road, and therefore Gateacre means 'the way to the hill of oaks'. This is also a reasonable assertion, however it is not without its problems. If, like Acrefield, the name does derive from Old Norse, then we would perhaps expect to see mention of it in one of its earlier forms, for example Gataclaw, Gatakelou or something similar. Yet, unlike the antecedent forms of Acrefield which are mentioned several times, no such precursor of Gateacre appears to have been recorded. Instead, the phrase 'the Gate Acre' appears in the court rolls of the 16th and 17th centuries fully anglicised and modernised.

Having studied the court rolls of Little Woolton closely, another more straightforward theory presents itself, in that 'Acre' was simply a suffix denoting an area of land[1]. Its use as such was very common in the 16th and 17th centuries. In times when the area was predominantly rural, parcels of land needed names by which they could be recognised and referred to. They were mostly given local or 'customary' names which were not necessarily permanent and could be subject to change through the generations. Pieces of land named after the owner or, quite often, the occupant – for example Lawrenson's Field, Holmes' meadow or Skillington's Hey – could see their names changed at the advent of a new occupier. Some of these names did embed themselves in the local psyche and a property could often retain the name of previous tenants long after they had died or moved on. Another way in which land was named was to reflect a physical feature, something which was on the land or nearby. Examples of this are the Mill Hey, the Old House Hey, the Brook Croft and the Bridge Meadow. As well as the terms croft, meadow, hey, close and field, the term 'acre' was used in a similar manner, and examples of this are plentiful. In Childwall there was the Score Acre, the Well Acre, the Four Acre, and the Eleven Acre, amongst others. In Much Woolton there was the Stony Acre, the Little Acre, the Four Acre, the Crown Acre, the Grange Acre, the Half Acre, and in Little Woolton there were the Carr Acre, the Little Cross Acre, the Five Acre and, of course, the Gate Acre. It therefore follows that the use of the name Gate Acre is consistent with this common practice of naming land.

So if the Gate Acre did refer to an area of land, where was it situated? It was clearly within the Little Woolton boundary, as the Little Woolton manor court had authority over its occupants. In the early 1600s the Halewood family are described as 'of the Gate Acre'. And what is described as Halewood's 'Little House' is said to be near 'the gate'. In the late 17th century this gate is referred to as the Smithy Gate (see Fig.10), and a gate is shown across Grange Lane near to Gateacre Brow on the Tithe map of 1848. This gate appears to have been something of a land mark, and was mentioned a number of times in the manorial records. It could arguably have been this gate that gave the Gate Acre its name. A survey of the commons or waste land of Much Woolton in 1658 also assists in locating the Gate Acre. The boundary of the commons is described as starting half way down the Out Lane, and then heading north to the Gate Acre. The boundary then went west up the Hill to a boundary stone (possibly the stone which still exists at the junction of Church Road and Reservoir Road on Woolton Hill – see fig 9). It can be reasonably posited that if the Gate Acre was an area of land, then it was the area that is situated on the corner of modern day Gateacre Brow and Grange Lane.

As development progressed around the Gate Acre, the settlement began to take on its name. Over time a handful of dwellings, a court house and a chapel were built and the 'the' was dropped. Eventually the name Gate Acre merged into its present name of Gateacre, and the settlement became a village in its own right, with its own identity. Because of its unique location straddling the township border, the village remained split between Much and Little Woolton until the old townships were dissolved in the 20th Century. Saying that, there was a bid to unify the village in the late 19th century.

In 1893 Gateacre separated from Childwall to form its own parish, with St Stephen's Church on Belle Vale Road becoming the parish church. The new parish of Gateacre incorporated all of the Little Woolton Township, as well as that part of Gateacre which lay in Much Woolton. In 1895, emboldened by the action of the church, the Little Woolton Urban Council made a bid to bring the part of Gateacre village which lay over the border under their control by a proposed annexation. However, the residents and owners of the properties in that part of the village protested strongly, preferring to stay within Much Woolton, and the bid collapsed. And so it remained that Gateacre was split between the two townships until after their incorporation into the city of Liverpool in 1913. Eventually the administration of the district was rearranged and the old Little Woolton and Much Woolton townships were broken up and made obsolete. Gateacre became its own suburb, and the suburbs, or wards, of Netherley and Belle Vale were created.

(Fig.11) The stone situated on Church Road, Woolton at the junction with Reservoir Road, which marks the ancient boundary of the Much Woolton and Little Woolton townships. This was once the open common land of the hill, Church Road not being constructed until after the 1805 Enclosures Act. There has been a stone at this location since at least 1658, but probably much earlier.

Notes:

[1]The term 'acre' used in this context did not refer to land which was only one statute acre in size, but was a general term like 'close' or 'croft'. Evidence of this can be seen in the fact that the Well Acre in Childwall was actually 3 acres in area, and the Score Acre was 2¼ acres.

CHILDWALL

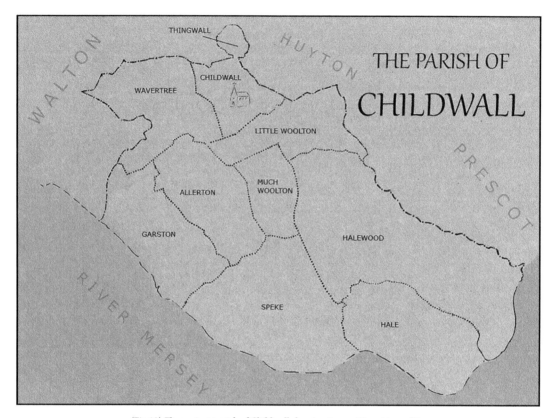

(Fig.12) *The ancient parish of Childwall showing its constituent townships*

Childwall is a township with a history closely related to that of Little Woolton. The township of Childwall should not be confused with the much larger *parish* of Childwall. The parish, which was an area of ecclesiastical administration, consisted of a number of townships including Wavertree, Much Woolton, Little Woolton, Garston, Allerton, Speke, Hale, Halewood, the hamlet of Thingwall, and Childwall itself. Township, often shortened to 'towne' in old records, is a term which is more or less obsolete today and denoted a subdivision of a parish which could contain one or perhaps several small settlements. The township of Childwall was moderately small, rural and sparsely populated, its defining feature for many years being the ancient church which served the whole parish. For clarity, whenever Childwall is mentioned from hereon it should be taken as referring to the township or village, and not the parish unless specifically stated.

Childwall appears in the Domesday Book of 1086 as 'Cildeuuelle', so it can be safely assumed that some kind of settlement already existed when King William's officials conducted their survey. There have been a number of different spellings of the name in the past, and a number of suggestions as to its origins. One has it that it is derived from the Old Norse for well field, 'kelda' being well and 'vollr' being field. Another that it is of Anglo Saxon origin, from 'cild' meaning child, and 'wella' meaning spring. There was at least one well near to the village centre, at the bottom of the aptly named Well Lane, as well as a natural spring, not far from the church, around which walls were constructed and which was known as the Monks' Bath. Either, or both, could easily have contributed to the naming of the settlement which became Childwall.

At the time of the Domesday Book there is mention of a priest at Childwall, which suggests there was a church or place of worship of some kind. This is supported by a record showing that in 1094 the church of Childwall was given by Roger de Poitou to the monks of St Martin of Séez. The church was rebuilt in the 12th century, but nothing in the current building can be dated to earlier than the 14th century, although there were reports that some 12th century stones were discovered while repairs were being made to the church in the Victorian era. The church has been continually improved and sections rebuilt and added over the centuries. Childwall's ancient church, which now goes by the name of All Saints, a relatively modern dedication, formed the focal point for the whole parish, though the settlement which grew up around it remained small. Even as late as 1907 Childwall was described as having 'an agreeable, park-like appearance, with plantations and pastures' and 'cultivated fields where crops of corn, turnips and potatoes are raised', and that 'there are but few dwellings, beside the hall and the houses which cluster about the church.'

While the church was an undoubted influence in Childwall, and held some of the land in and around the churchyard and rectory, much of the township or manor was in private hands. In the 12th century, the manors of Childwall and Allerton were acquired by Albert Grelley the baron of Manchester, and much of the land remained in the possession of the Grelley family until 1473. In 1212 Richard de Lathom also held lands in Childwall, which passed down through his family line, and in 1339 Edward III granted Thomas de Lathom a grant of free warren (permission to hunt rabbits and small game) in the lands he held in Childwall. By 1473 the whole of the manor lands that were not held by the church were in the ownership of Thomas Lord Stanley, who in 1485 became the first Earl of Derby. Apart from the period between 1596 and 1614, the Manor of Childwall remained in the hands of the Earls of Derby until seized by parliament after the English Civil War. Thereafter it was owned by a series of wealthy individuals which included Henry Nevill and Anthony Samwell, Elizabeth Bagnall, and from 1659 the Legay family. It was eventually acquired by Isaac Greene in 1718, and it was via marriage and inheritance within the Greene family that the Manor of Childwall, like that of Little Woolton, came into the ownership of Lord Salisbury.

Following the manorial pattern, Childwall had a manor house, or capital messuage, as it would have been referred to. Prior to the building of Childwall Hall in around 1720, the manor house of the township was Childwall House, which stood at the bottom of Well Lane. The house was situated conveniently close to the well, from which Well Lane, and quite possibly Childwall itself, derive their name. Though the old manor house and well are both long gone and built over with modern housing, Well Lane still exists, though it is now intersected by Gateacre Park Drive. Childwall was only one of the many manors owned by the Earls of Derby, and there is no evidence that the Earls ever resided at Childwall House. Rather it was leased to a succession of wealthy tenants, who themselves often had under tenants.

In 1595 William Earl of Derby granted the lease for the manor of Childwall, along with Childwall House, to Baptist Hycks, a merchant from London. Hycks retained the lease until, in the 1620s the manor house and estate were leased from the Earl by Gabriel Haughton, and, following his death, his son Hugh. However, at the conclusion of the English Civil War in 1651 the lands in the hands of James Earl of Derby, which included Childwall, were seized by Parliament. In 1652 a survey of Childwall was conducted on behalf of the ruling republican government in preparation for its sale to wealthy supporters of the Parliamentarian cause. In the survey, Childwall House was described as a capital messuage[1] or manor house, consisting of two buildings called the new and the old buildings, containing a hall, kitchen, buttery, and five other lower rooms and six upper rooms. One large barn, two shippons[2], one kiln house, one garden, one orchard, one large fold yard, and one yard called the Rye Yard, all of which covered an area of four acres. There was a large area of land which was rented along with Childwall House which covered an area of approximately 81 acres. The House and associated lands were at this time in the tenure of Isabell Haughton, widow of Hugh Haughton.

(Fig.13) A sketch c1810 by J.Hindley from the Binns Collection. Marked in pencil as 'Childwall Hall' this is, in fact, Childwall House which stood at the bottom of Well Lane. At the time this sketch was made, Childwall Hall was the imposing, turreted edifice built by Bamber Gascoyne. A mishmash of architectural styles in this picture, Childwall House was the township's first manor house and was itself enlarged and added to over the years. The part of the house to the right is of 16th century style, with what appear to be stone mullioned windows. The end of the house to the far left has architectural similarities with the Abbey Inn, and may have been added around the same time the inn was rebuilt in the first part of the 18th century, possibly when Isaac Greene lived here. Used with permission of Liverpool Record Office, Liverpool Libraries.

The Haughton family also had tenancy of Childwall's windmill, which stood upon the common land of Childwall Hill between modern day Childwall Lane and the Childwall Park Avenue estate. Today the site is occupied by housing and the former grounds of Childwall Hall, but in

1642, when the mill is first recorded, the area was open fields, and the area between Childwall Lane and the mill known as Milne Brow. The mill was referred to at this time as the 'new milne', implying it was newly built, possibly on the site of an older mill, and was granted by the Earl of Derby to Gabriel Haughton. The windmill survived the rest of the 17th century, under various tenants, but was gone by the early 1700s.

After a flurry of different owners between 1655 and 1659, Childwall and Little Woolton manors were acquired by Peter and Isaac Legay. The Legays began to make their mark upon Childwall, and revived, or even possibly instigated, the Childwall manorial court. It was at this time that Well Lane, until this point an informal path from the church to Childwall House, was recognised as a legitimate lane or 'way'. In 1659, the court officers of new Lord of the Manor took stock of the lanes, highways and byways running through his lands. Three of the local tenants and land holders, Henry Orme, James Abbot and Edmund Wainwright (licensee of the inn that was to become the Abbey) gave information to the court that there had always been a way from Mercer's House next to the church, through Mercer's Fold and down to the well and Childwall House. The way was referred to locally as Mercer's Lane, and like many of the roads running through the manor was gated at the top. The recognition by the court of the ancient way as a formal lane meant it could be supervised by the court's officers, and that they could order the occupants of the land through which it passed to carry out maintenance and repairs when it was deemed necessary. Mercer's Lane eventually became known as Well Lane, the name it still bears today.

Interestingly, Score Lane, an old route from Childwall to Broad Green, was also named differently in ancient times. In the records of the 17th century it is referred to as the Pyke or Pike Lane and was gated at each end. Like Well Lane, and other lanes in the township, it was not strictly a public road, or 'King's Highway', but belonged to the lord of the manor. Being an ancient right of way, access by the public was permitted, but there were controls in place. Foot traffic and access by horse or small carts was generally accepted, but the driving of large carriages drawn by teams of horses was not. Such use would damage and churn up the rudimentary road surface, usually a mix of sand and stones, requiring frequent and costly repairs. On the occasion that team owners did drive along the lord's lanes contrary to local decree, they would be liable to be brought before the manor court and fined. As well as preventing cattle and livestock from straying, the gates at the ends of these roads seemed to perform a number of functions. They prevented uncontrolled access, as well as distinguishing the point at which King's Highway ended and the private road began. They also indicated the point at which land holders took over responsibility for road maintenance. The maintenance of the gates themselves fell to the tenants of the land upon which they were sited. The gate which was situated outside the Abbey Inn (not called by this name at the time) was erected in 1661 by Edmund Wainwright, the occupant and licensee, on the order of the manorial court. Wainwright was ordered to make a '*yeate*' (gate) at the end of his house and to maintain it, and also to repair and maintain the wall from the gate to the Church Ashfield. In 1670, Childwall tenant William Ellison was ordered by the manor court to repair his fences along the Pyke Lane, and to '*set a yeate at the end of the lane*'. In 1697, Hugh Vaux and Francis Bailey were ordered to repair and reset the latches and catches on the gates at either end of the Pyke Lane, and Hugh Vaux was ordered to put the Pyke Lane in good repair '*so far as it lies against his ground*'. In contrast to the manorial lord's lanes, it was the responsibility of every resident of the township to assist in maintaining and repairing the public highway. The town's inhabitants would be ordered to transport sand and stones in their carts, and to perform work as and when the supervisors of the highway saw fit. To not do so would attract a fine. Eventually, all surviving thoroughfares in the area became public roads, though for some of the roads in Childwall that did not occur until as late as the 20th century.

(Fig.14) One of the earliest depictions of Childwall from c1810 by J. Hindley, showing the church and the Abbey Inn. In the foreground is the common land where the ancient market was held and which was allocated to the church after the local Enclosures Act of 1805[4]. By 1813 it was part of the vicarage grounds and was walled in. Used with permission of the Liverpool Record Office, Liverpool Libraries.

One of the most important figures in the history of both Childwall and Little Woolton was Isaac Greene. Greene was a lawyer who was born in 1678 and baptised at St Nicholas' Church in Liverpool. In the early 18th century, he set about acquiring several complete manors in the Lancashire area, including Childwall and Little Woolton. He also purchased the manors of Much Woolton, Wavertree, Everton, West Derby, Hale and Eltonhead. As a lawyer often tasked with sorting out the affairs of the land owning gentry, he found himself ideally placed to identify and take advantage of any opportunities to purchase land and estates that may have arisen. Greene was also related to the Legay family, and was the nephew of Katherine Legay, heiress to the manors of Childwall and Woolton. In 1703 he became the steward of the manor court of Childwall and Little Woolton, which no doubt made the acquisition of those manors from his aunt much easier, and it was in 1718 that he completed the purchase of the two manors. Unlike a number of the previous Lords of the Childwall Manor, Greene had decided to live in the township and, having initially resided at Childwall House, enclosed a portion of the commons to build the first Childwall Hall which was completed before 1724. Greene also enclosed some of the Little Woolton commons, building a summer house on Woolton

Hill and a tavern near to modern day Woolton Road. Although he was quite keen to place his own stamp on the locale where he resided, neither his Hall, Summer House nor tavern on Woolton Road lasted more than a few decades before being either demolished or rebuilt. Isaac Greene died in 1749 during an excursion to Scarborough. His daughter, Mary Greene, inherited Childwall and Little Woolton. It was Mary who married Bamber Gascoyne[3], who by default became lord of the manor. Hence, through their descendants, the manors came into the ownership of the Marquesses of Salisbury, with whom they remained well into the 20th century.

(Fig.15) Isaac Greene (1679-1749), Lord of the Manors of Childwall and Little Woolton from 1718, and builder of the first Childwall Hall.

Notes:

[1]A 'messuage' was a house or dwelling with land and outbuildings, and a 'capital messuage' was literally the capital or main house of the manor. The capital messuage, or manor house, was usually where the lord of lady of the manor lived. In later centuries the term came to be used to describe any large mansion house within its own grounds or estate.

[2]A 'shippon' is an archaic term for a cattle shed, and is a term which was still in use into the early 20th century.

[3]Bamber Gascoyne (1725-1791) was an English politician and Member of Parliament. Gascoyne married Mary Greene in January 1757* and as her husband became Lord of the Manors of Childwall and Little Woolton. The estates were inherited by their son, also called Bamber Gascoyne, whose daughter and heir, Frances Mary Gascoyne, married James Cecil, 2nd Marquess of Salisbury, in 1821. The manors of Childwall and Little Woolton therefore came into Salisbury's possession. The son of James and Frances, Robert Gascoyne-Cecil,

became 3rd Marquess of Salisbury, inheriting Childwall from his father. Lands in Childwall and Little Woolton (as well as elsewhere) remained under the ownership of the Salisburys until the 20th century.

* Some sources state 1756, however this is due to a retention of the Julian calendar in some quarters, though officially it had been superseded by the Gregorian calendar in 1752. Prior to 1752 in England the New Year commenced on 25th March, ending on 24th March 12 months later.

[4]Abridged for brevity. The full title of the 1805 Act was 'An Act for Inclosing Lands in the Manors or Townships of Childwall, Great Woolton and Little Woolton, in the Parish of Childwall, in the County Palatine of Lancaster.'

THE MANOR COURT OF LITTLE WOOLTON AND CHILDWALL

The manorial system of land ownership, tenancy and governance has its roots in Saxon times and was retained and further developed by the Normans after 1066. The manor was the basic unit of feudal lordship, usually under the ownership and control of a local lord, and this system persisted, albeit subject to change and development, throughout the medieval and post-medieval periods.

There was much variance in how various manors were arranged and managed around the country. As well as having to abide by the laws of the land, manors also had their own customary laws, the modern-day equivalent of which would be the local byelaw. The governance of the manor was achieved through the local manor courts, by which the lord exercised his jurisdiction usually through a steward. Though the courts were held in the current Lord or Lady of the Manor's name, they very rarely attended the court in person, certainly in the case of Little Woolton and Childwall.

The earliest court records that survive for Little Woolton are from 1547, when the manor was in the hands of William Norris of Speke. Later the manor was purchased by William Earl of Derby, and then, following the English Civil War, under the control of owners such as the Legay family, and Isaac Greene.

It was common for manorial courts to be held at the manor house. Given the specific makeup of Little Woolton and Childwall, the location of the manorial court for those areas changed over the years. The early courts of William Norris would have been held at the Lee, the Holt not yet having been built. After the building of the Holt house by William Brettargh in 1583, and the subsequent acquisition of the Lee by the Ireland family who chose to reside elsewhere, the Holt grew in prominence. By the early 1600s, the manorial court was being held at the Holt, which was then the residence of the steward of the court, Edward Stockley. Following the acquisition of the manors of Little Woolton and Childwall by Peter Legay, the location of the court changed again.

In 1652, following the English Civil War, the officers of the State arrived in Childwall to take stock. What they found was a manor with no court, no elected officers and no form of local governance other than that provided by the Church. When they made enquiries with local people they were informed that no manorial court had been held in Childwall for over two decades, though in truth it is possible that one had never been held at all. Law and order, rather than being overseen by locally elected officials, had been kept by men in the employ of the Earl of Derby. When he became lord of the manors of Childwall and Little Woolton in 1659, Peter Legay revived the Childwall court, but decided to combine it with the Little Woolton court, holding a joint court for both townships. A new location for the court was required that was more centrally located than the Brettargh Holt, and so a new court house was built on a piece of common waste land in Gateacre. This court house would eventually become part of the Black Bull public house. The manorial court was held here until the early 1700s, at which time the court for Childwall and Little Woolton townships was split into two and held at separate locations, though initially still under the same steward. The court house was acquired by the Orme family of the Grange, and the ancient Little Woolton town chest, which was used to store important documents such as the court rolls, land and property documents, and the town's funds, was moved temporarily to Orme's Grange on Grange Lane. In 1704, the court ordered that '*the constables of the towne do immediately repair the towne chest with locks and keys and remove it from the Grange to the Holt*'. Initially, the newly separated Childwall court was held at the house of Eleanor Abbot, the inn that became known as the Abbey. The Little Woolton court moved back to the Holt, with the small court house in Gateacre falling out of use. With records of the manor courts after the early 1700s becoming less detailed, it is unclear how long Childwall's court was held at Ellenor Abbot's house. It is likely that after the building of the first Childwall Hall by Isaac Greene, the court was accommodated there, though no records of Childwall's manor court seem to have survived after 1715.

THE OFFICERS OF THE COURT

Most years the manorial court sat just twice per annum, in April and in October. In some years, a third and even a fourth court was held as occasion demanded, though this was rare. There are even years when, for reasons unknown, no court sat at all, only for proceedings to commence again a year or two later, picking up where they had left off when it had last been held.

In terms of how the manor court worked, all land owners and principal tenants of the manor were obliged to contribute or 'do service' to the court. The most prominent would sit on the jury, and be prepared to be elected as officers of the court for the year. Any tenant, including those of high status, who failed to attend the court or to do their due service would be fined. As well as court duty, inhabitants were also expected to carry out labour on behalf of the Lord of the Manor, non-compliance with which likewise attracted a fine. In 1637, Richard Lawrenson was fined 2 shillings for '*neglecting the lord's service with hand labour of two days*', while James Halewood was fined 4 shillings for neglecting to carry out 4 days hand labour on behalf of the Lord of the Manor. Of course, both men would have been expected to send a representative, or under tenant, to do the actual labour on their behalf.

The court dealt with issues of tenure and inheritance of land and property, the regulation of communal trade and agriculture, and the settling of disputes such as debts, minor damage and trespass. The court also had the power to deal with minor criminal matters and misdemeanours, though serious matters would be dealt with by the appropriate criminal court or assizes. Yet the manorial court was not merely a punitive mechanism, and often worked on behalf of the local residents. In 1686 the concerns of local farmers were addressed when it was ordered that '*if any inhabitant within the township of Little Woolton shall kill or destroy any old magpies or jays within the said township they shall have for every each magpie or jay three half pence allowed by the said township*'. Such birds were considered a pest, and harmful to crops in particular.

The local manor court also had responsibility for the regulation and supervision of the local licensed premises, generally termed 'alehouses'. These establishments could vary in size and stature from fully fledged inns, to small country quaffing houses, but were governed by the same regulations and licensing requirements.

The officers of the court were elected on an annual basis, and had their own specific responsibilities. They were expected to summons, or 'present', to the jury those inhabitants of the town who had transgressed against the laws or rules of the manor. These officers had titles such as 'burleymen', 'hill lookers', 'fire lookers', 'leylayers', 'surveyors' or 'supervisors of the highway', and 'ale tasters', also sometimes referred to as 'alefounders'. There was also a town constable, or sometimes two, and a town bailiff. A brief descriptions of the roles and responsibilities of the officers of Little Woolton and Childwall are as follows:

Constable – The constable was appointed from amongst the land owners or chief tenants of the township and was responsible for overseeing general order. The office of constable was not the paid occupation we are familiar with now, rather its incumbent was elected annually and could be a different individual or individuals each year. He, or they, had the authority of the lord of the manor to present people to the manor court for minor misdemeanours, profane language, minor assaults or 'tussels', and other acts deemed unacceptable at the time. As part of their duties, the constables conducted what were termed as privi or privy searches. These searches involved the search of any place in the township where the constables believed they may find rogues, vagabonds, or idle or disorderly persons. It seems such a search was conducted in Little Woolton four times per year as a way of rounding up and dealing with undesirables. As well as the regular, scheduled privisearches, there was another type of search, called a 'hue and cry', which was a response to an unforeseen occurrence. In the event of perhaps a robbery or other violent crime being reported to them, the constables would enlist the assistance of men from the community to help them search for and apprehend the culprits. The requisite number of men would be gathered together in a 'muster' before setting about their task. This obligation was not always popular with the local townsfolk, as shown in the Little Woolton court rolls of 1640, when Ellin Fazakerley was presented before the court for *'giving evile words to the constable when he gave Rafe Fazakerley her husband warninge to goe unto the general muster'*. She was fined 12 pence for her trouble. There were obviously occasions when the untrained elected constables felt they needed more substantial assistance than a muster of local citizens could provide, perhaps when dealing with a particularly ruthless group of felons operating in the area, or a more significant threat to general order. In October 1627, the Little Woolton court ordered that all inhabitants of the township over the age of eighteen years contribute 12 pence towards the hiring of a soldier when it was deemed necessary. The soldier would be able to assist the constable during a privy search or 'hue and cry', and may even have engaged in some sort of patrol or guard duty as required. It seems there were occasions when the hiring of a soldier to assist the township was indeed deemed necessary. In April 1651, when the usual names of the landowners and chief tenants are listed in the court rolls, the very last entry reads *'John Johnson a soldier in service'*.

The admission of new people into the township of Little Woolton was tightly controlled, and in 1637 the manor court ordered that *'no man shall receive a tenant into this manor except he give sufficient security according to the law to prevent the town harm'*. The evidence of the entries in the rolls suggests that this was particularly applicable to persons of lower status, and quite often the permission of the Constables was required before a house or cottage could be let out to a new tenant. There appears to have been less obstruction and controls in place in relation to the transfer, buying and leasing of properties amongst more wealthy and higher status individuals, and these transactions were relatively commonplace. This could be seen as a way of controlling the movement of lower class undesirables or 'riff raff' in and around the township.

Though they were technically unpaid, the constables could claim expenses from the towne's coffers. In 1709 the Little Woolton court saw fit to make it clear to the constables for that year, William Webster and Thomas Knowles, the extent of the expenses they were allowed to claim. In an order made by the court it was proclaimed that *'the constables of the towne shall have 10 shillings per annum to beare their expenses and 6 pence a time for the four privisearches and the like for every huw and cry and no more'*. The order of the court suggests that constables from previous years had perhaps been claiming more than they were entitled to for carrying out their duties.

Bailiff – The bailiff worked on behalf of the steward of the court to collect any fines levied. Undoubtedly an unpopular role, he would have come up against a degree of resistance on occasion, similar to how modern day bailiffs might. In 1625 Richard Lyon of Little Woolton was fined 12d for *'giving multiplication of words to the lord's bailiff of this manor'*. The meaning of this can be reasonably guessed at, with Lyon probably trying to lie or sweet talk his way out of paying his fine. The bailiff was also in charge of the township's pinfold, and would be responsible for impounding cattle which had strayed or was subject of a dispute, and the release of which could be secured upon payment of a fee or fine.

Burleymen – The burleymen, sometimes referred to as barleymen or burlamen, were appointed to assist the constable in matters arising relating to trespass, damage and encroachment. They were also responsible for inspecting the condition of the hedges, fences and ditches, which divided different pieces of land and separated land from the highway. They would instruct land owners or tenants to construct or repair their fences, and to maintain or trim their hedges when necessary. In 1651 Elizabeth Whitfield and Edward Knowles were fined by the manor court for not *'making by their hedges according to the burlamen's command'*. Not cutting a hedge or scouring a ditch would attract a fine from the court, and was a common occurrence in the 17th century.

Hill Lookers – Before modern day development changed the face of the area, the defining physical feature of Little Woolton and Childwall was the hill. Part of the hill was in also in Much Woolton, but the 'hill lookers' of Little Woolton and Childwall had duties relating to the management of the part of the Hill in their townships. Most of the hill of Little Woolton was open common or waste land at the time, but activities that could be undertaken upon it were still controlled and regulated. The hill lookers would have undertaken activities such as watching out for straying cattle, people grazing their livestock on the hill, or people hunting or taking game and other resources, such as wood and turf or turves. People from the town were only allowed to take modest amounts of such materials, and only at certain times of the year. It was particularly frowned upon for people from nearby townships to graze cattle, or take resources from the hill. In 1640, John Glover of Roby was presented to the court by the hill lookers and fined 5 shillings for trespassing with sheep on the common of Little Woolton, and for leaving them there. The same year the court rolls record *'two ewe sheep as strayes beinge taken up by Thomas Justice and William Abbot being hill lookers and delivered unto the lord's baliffe.'* The sheep were kept in the pinfold pending collection by their owner John

Broughton, who was duly fined 6s 6d. At the October court of 1658, the hill lookers George Highfield and Thomas Justice presented Thomas Bell of Childwall before the court for 'getting heath upon the lord's part of the Hill', and Richard Miller, servant to William Cockett, for 'carrying it away'. They were fined 4 shillings between them. The role of hill looker tended to be given to those inhabitants who lived on or near the foot of the hill and which made them ideally placed to carry out their duties.

Fire Lookers – The role of the 'fire lookers' of the Little Woolton manor may seem obvious, but it was somewhat more involved than merely looking out for fires. In the 15th century timber chimneys had been outlawed in England, but the majority of the buildings built before the latter half of the 17th century were mostly timber framed, with lath and plaster walls, thatched roofs and straw on the floors. Evidence of this in Little Woolton can be found in the court rolls of 1690 when Thomas Naylor was order to 'put his housing in good repair with wattle and daub'. The threat of fire was very real and ever present, as it would spread quickly and easily. As far back as the time of William the Conqueror, fires had been required to be extinguished at night as a means of fire prevention, and this requirement continued for many centuries afterwards. The manorial court of 17th century Little Woolton appointed officers to ensure that the inhabitants of the area extinguished their fires at the allotted time each evening. The 'fire lookers' were also charged with ensuring that all inhabitants had made the necessary preparations to deal with any fires that did happen to break out, with ready access to water and/or sand. Finally, they would be expected to inspect the dwellings within the township to ensure that no chimneys were defective and therefore likely to be a fire hazard. In 1693, the fire lookers for that year, Henry Halewood and Henry Webster, reported to the court that 'we have made enquirie that all persons be sufficiently provided for fire and we know of none unprovided'.

Aletasters – The alefounders or aletasters were appointed by the court to ensure that any ale and bread sold by the innkeepers of the township was of a sufficient standard and measure, or 'assize'. Prior to the advent of the large commercial breweries, which began to be established in the area in the late 18th and 19th centuries, alehouses had brew houses on site or nearby where the ale sold at the house would be brewed. The quality of the ale from house to house was therefore of varying and sometimes questionable quality. The aletasters had a duty to ensure that alehouse keepers weren't selling ale that was sub-standard or unhealthy. As well as the quality of their ale, alehouse keepers and inn keepers could break the assize of ale by selling ale in too small a measure, at too high a price, or both. The same scrutiny was applied to the selling of bread. Licensees were presented to the court on a frequent and regular basis for 'breaking the assize of bread and ale.' The aletasters would also report back to the court on other licensing matters, including the selling of ale without a licence, or keeping unlawful gaming in the house in contravention to the law. It appears that it was not just alehouse keepers who were inspected, but bakers also. In 1623 John Highfield, baker of Little Woolton, was fined 3 shillings for 'selling browne bread under the weight of the market'.

Ley layers – were connected with the assessment and levying of fines and other township expenses on the inhabitants of the manor. The other officers would make take their findings to the leylayers before each court and they would set the fine to be paid for each misdemeanour or order broken. This in itself did not appear to be too taxing a duty, as the sums which people were fined, or 'amerced', for certain offences seemed to be fairly standard and did not change from year to year. More importantly, the leylayers were responsible for keeping records of fines levied, paid and owed.

Surveyors/supervisors of the Roads/Highways – as the title may suggest, the supervisors of the highways were responsible for the general upkeep of the roads running through the township. They would report to the court as to whether the lanes and highways of the township were in acceptable condition and traversable and had the authority of the court to instruct land owners whose lands the roads passed through or near, to repair them with sand and stones as required. They would also instruct landowners or occupants to lay flags or paving at certain places as deemed necessary. Anybody failing to abide by the instructions of the supervisors would be liable to a fine, and a further order to carry out the work. Not even the most wealthy and influential land owners were exempt from their obligations in this respect. In 1622 Anne Brettargh, owner of the Holt Manor house and estate, was fined 24 pence by the court for not bringing paving slabs and stones to the highway, as were neighbouring land owners Thomas Naylor and John Bridge. The same year, Thomas Halewood, George Brookes and Richard Brookes were fined 6 pence each for *'not coming to worke at the hee way with a spade'*.

THE CONCERNS OF THE COURT

It is evident that the manorial court functioned in a similar way to modern courts, with witnesses called to give evidence having sworn an oath on a bible to tell the truth. In 1682, Mary Orme found herself fined 6s and 6d when it was recorded by the court that *'upon information upon oath given before us we present Mary Orme of Little Woolton as a common breaker of her neighbors hedges and who kills and destroys her neighbors goods.'* In 1688 it is written in the rolls that *'upon information upon oath we present Richard Abbott for raising discords amongst his neighbours by sowing seditious words and moving of false tales to the great defamation of severall persons of repute and good fame'.* Abbott was fined 13s and 4d.

While more serious misdemeanours would be brought before the assize court in Wigan, minor felonies could be dealt with by the local manor court. Fights and assaults, or 'tussels', between the townspeople were a regular occurrence, and resulted in the punishment of both parties. If blood was drawn, then the fine was greater. While virtually all punishments at this local level took the form of a fine, other methods were available if deemed appropriate, such as stocks, cucking stool or bridle. In 1620, Ellizabeth Fletcher was presented before the court for *'feloniously taking a silver spoon'* belonging to Thomas Orme of the Lee, and she was deferred to be punished at the discretion of William Norres, in whose name, as deputy to the Earl of Derby, the court was being held at that time. It does not state what punishment was meted out by Norres in this case, but a fine does not appear to have been levied. It could be that Fletcher spent some time in the town stocks for her troubles. In 1632, Elizabeth Gleast was found to have stolen from the garden of Robert Williamson, and taken fruit from William Gill's hedge. As a punishment she was *'to bee stocked for a quarter of an oure'*. The case of Elizabeth Gleast is a rare instance of the stocks being recorded as being used, though in the court rolls of 1635, it was noted that while the town stocks were in good repair, there was no whipping stock or cucking stool.

Another example of minor crime being dealt with locally was an incident which happened at the Grange on Grange Lane, the house of Henry Orme. In 1658 Thomas Gill was presented before the manorial court for 'trespassing and taking a buck forth of Henry Orme's kitchen'. The jury of the court also presented Thomas Gill, James Harrison and Richard Pickering for 'carrying the buck to Marjorie Gill's house and their eating it' as well as Marjorie Gill for 'suffering it to be eaten in her house.' On this occasion the offending parties were dealt with by way of a fine, though this incident says more perhaps about the class divide, and the gulf between the haves and the have nots. The difference in wealth between near neighbours is highlighted by the fact that those involved were compelled to steal from the bountifully stocked kitchen of the local landowner not for commercial gain, but to eat.

A typical example of other matters that could come before the manor court can be seen in the entries in the rolls on 3rd May 1637. On this day several local tenants appeared before the jury. Roger Crosse, a servant to Mr Rigbie of the Hutt in Halewood was fined 6 shillings and 6 pence for 'strykinge and drawing blood upon the bodie of William Houlgreave' within the Little Woolton manor. William Tilslaye of Huyton was fined 12d for abusing Richard Walton with 'evill and corrupte words'. Alis Harrison was fined for trespassing upon the land of Richard Sefton with her cattle. Other matters before the court in 1637 included William Sadler being ordered to repave and make a 'pitt' he had made in the highway 'sensible' so that the king's laypeople could pass by without danger, on pain of 20 shillings.

As well as obvious acts such as assaults and petty thefts, imprudent words and actions could draw the displeasure of the court in the parochial Stuart era Little Woolton. In 1629, Henry Halewood, the son of Thomas Halewood, was fined 3 shillings 4 pence for 'enticing and persuading John Cockett to the committing of serious felonies, the said John not yielding thereunto'. In 1633, Elizabeth Whitfield, wife of John Whitfield was presented and fined 3s 4d for 'giving unseemly speeches against her mother in law viz: calling her hore and other unseemly words against the steward of this manor' while John Whitfield was presented before the same court for 'going abroad in the night att inconvenient times, verie suspiciously'. He was fined 3s 4d.

There were clearly some things which the local court felt they could not adequately deal with, and about which they sought the authority of the higher assize court. In 1649, 44 of the principle inhabitants of Little Woolton signed a complaint which they lodged with the assize court at Wigan against local woman Elin Wild. The nature of the complaint was that 'Elin Wild of Little Woolton in the county of Lancaster is a verie bad and lewd woman' and that she was 'kepeing a comon baudie house and receiving different women's husbands and also a very bad woman in her house' which was 'to the great griffe and trouble of her nebours and to the disturbance of the peace of the towne'. The result of the complaint and the fate of Elin Wild is not known.

The impact of the Interregnum, or Cromwellian era, of 1649 to 1660 was felt within the Little Woolton Township. This is apparent in some of the offences brought before the manor court in that period. In the October court of 1657, John Knowles, John Linaker, Richard Ireland the flayman, Edward Halewood, Richard Harrison, John Baledon, William Ashcroft, Thomas Wainwright, and William Webster, all of Little Woolton, were presented for 'playing att the nine peges or cales upon the Lordes Day'. This is a reference to the playing of a game akin to skittles, which evolved from the medieval game of Kayles or Loggats, and all the men were fined 2 shillings each for playing on a Sunday. The same year, James Harrison, Thomas Gill, John Knowles the younger son of Edward Knowles, and John Boden a miller of Halewood, were fined 2 shillings each for '*playing att the cappellett*' on the Lord's Day, 'the cappellett' possibly being a card game of sorts. The fact that these offences come to prominence in this period indicates an increased ardour within the manor for dealing with religious infringements of this nature.

Another indication of the sensitivities of the time can be found in the court rolls of the same year. An order of the court decreed that '*no inhabitant within the towne shall harbour a woman called the wise woman in the paine of five shillings a night*'. This may seem a strange order, and one might be inclined to ask why a woman should be excluded from staying in Little Woolton solely on the basis of her wisdom. However, in Cromwellian England the term 'wise woman' had a different inference. This was a society steeped in superstitions, and sensitive in particular to perceived witchcraft. While the court did not outright condemn the said woman as being versed in dark practices, they were clearly suspicious of someone holding such a title, and, erring on the side of caution, were keen to ensure that no one gave her lodging.

THE CONTROL OF WOMEN

If the distrust of the 'wise woman', and its veiled suggestion of witchcraft, is indicative of the religious mores of the time, it is also emblematic of the position of women in that period. In over 150 years of records, from the first listings of the local court in the late 16th century, up until records begin to peter out in the mid-18th century, not a single officer of the court or jury member is a woman. And in the lists of chief tenants and land owners over the same period and longer, the vast majority were men. Women did appear in the lists, but only as widows who had inherited property from their late husband, or unmarried heiresses. When a woman did appear as a land owner, the word 'widow' would usually follow her name by way of qualification or explanation. Bereaved men did not require the same qualification it seems, as nowhere does 'widower' follow their names. As soon as a woman married, or in the case of a widow remarried, their inherited estates became the property of their husband. Such conditions even applied to the wealthiest women. Several women became 'Lady of the Manor' upon the death of their husband or father, but upon marriage 'lordship' transferred to their new husband.

As well as women being subjugated by societal conventions, there is evidence of the control of women in the way the all-male manorial court acted. There are numerous examples of women being treated differently than men. While men could be 'rogues' and 'vagabonds', terms which were disparaging but which didn't disempower them or detract from their manhood, women were described as 'misguided' or 'strange'. In 1629, Thomas Halewood '*the blinde man*' was fined by the court for '*harboringe a wanderinge rogue, and one Ann Cooke being a misguided woman*'. In another illustration of the status of women, the 1634 court ordered that no inhabitant of the manor shall '*take and receive into anie house a woman called by the name of the wiffe of Henrie Blackmore's wiffe, in the paine of 20 shillings*'. In this instance there isn't even a mention of the woman's name, she is merely referred to as 'Henrie Blackmore's wife', tantamount to being his property, and clearly not free to go where she pleased. Also that year, Henrie Halewood of the Gate Acre was fined 6 shillings for '*keeping a misguided woman in his house*'. In 1635 Edward Knowle was fined 6 shillings and 8 pence for also keeping a '*mysgyded woman*' in his house. There is a clear inference regarding prostitution in this term, and prostitution and alehouses were commonly linked in this era. The word 'misguided' takes away any notion of self-determinism, or even victimisation, from the women in question and instead suggests they were unable to conduct themselves in a proper manner without guidance. In 1637 Gwen Halewood, an inn keeper, was fined for '*harbouring two strange women*', and also for '*entertaining a strange woman in her house being suspected for a lewde woman*'. Halewood was fined 3s and 4d for the last offence, and was fined a further 10s for keeping the woman in her house having been warned by the constables to send her away. The control over women in childbirth is also evident when, in 1647, Richard Helsbie was fined 3s and 4d for '*suffering a basterd to bee borne att his house*'. It is unclear where the woman was supposed to give birth.

THE DEMISE OF THE MANORIAL COURT

In April 1693 matters at the Little Woolton and Childwall manor court came to a head. For several years previously, there had been no presentments made to the court by its officers. Being essentially accused of neglect, all officers were given an order by the steward to make presentments to the court, or, if they could not, to at least make a negative report. The officers were themselves then punished for their neglect. The aletasters for Little Woolton, Samuel Knowles and Richard Walton, were each fined 1 shilling for '*not bringing in a presentment*', while Childwall's ale tasters, William Carter and David Ellison, who also held the office of burleymen and fire lookers, were similarly fined for the same dereliction of duty. Thereafter, the presentments to the court began again, if only for the officers to report that '*we have naught to present*'. At the October 1693 court an entry in the rolls reads, '*we the hill lookers Nathan Rathbone and Henry Halewood present Henry Hoake and John Lunt and John Norris for getting heath and gorse of Little Woolton Hill as witness our hands. John Boulton of Wavertree for burning of fern on Little Woolton Hill. Write to Mr Legay about the fine before collected vis Henry Hoake, John Lunt and John Norris. John Boulton to pay.*' In the end all men were fined 6s 8d each. A report on 26th December 1693 by the hill looker for Childwall, Richard Foster, states, '*Richard Foster hill looker has made inquiry for wavs and strays within Childwall but find none and further I have not to present. There is none out of our towne that has got any turfe on our hill that I know of.*'

In 1694 the manor court ordered the constables of Little Woolton to provide a cucking stool and a bridle, and also build a shooting butt, as it had been recognised that the township was lacking such apparatus. A cucking stool, also known as a stool of repentance, was a device used for punishing disorderly persons, scolds and dishonest tradesmen. It was a stool to which the offending party could simply be tied for a period of time, paraded about the town or immersed in water. They would usually be naked for purposes of humiliation. A bridle was used to punish and humiliate mainly women who were seen to be rude, nags or scolds and consisted of a framework which enclosed the head with a bar or gag which fit into the mouth. The fact that Little Woolton did not have these items available indicated that such punishments had not been used in the township in recent years. The shooting butt, which was also required to be provided, was an earthen bank used to support a target for shooting practice. In the court of 1695, the Little Woolton constables were found not to have provided the cucking stool and were fined 3 shillings and 4 pence each, though it appears that the scold's bridle had been procured. In 1696 it was the township of Childwall that was found wanting, when the constables were taken to task for not having a cucking stool, pillory, bridle or whip.

As the end of the century drew near, presentments for offences dwindled. In 1697, John Norres, hill looker for Childwall, was fined for not bringing in any presentments to court, and the Childwall aletasters, Robert Hutchin and John Houlden, were similarly fined. Despite the best efforts of the court to have the misdemeanours of the inhabitants reported to them, most of its time became occupied with ensuring land owners and tenants kept their ditches clear and their hedges and fences in good repair. In 1698, Timothy Helsby, constable for Childwall reported that *'our stockes and rogues post are in good repair our high wayes are in good repair our hedges and ditches nere the high ways are kept cut and scoured and further I have not to present'*.

The last presentments of alehouse keepers was in 1699, when the licensees of Little Woolton and Childwall were all presented for breaking the assize of bread and ale. Thereafter most presentment reports were of a negative nature, except for the occasional person caught taking turf from the hill when they shouldn't have. In 1714, Thomas Tatlocke, hill looker of Childwall, was fined for neglecting his duty, and, interestingly, Henry Longworth and John Tenant of Childwall were fined 6s and 8d for travelling in the snow!

The entries in the rolls of Little Woolton and Childwall manorial court in their 16th to early 18th century heyday help to paint a fairly vivid picture of local life in that era. Many of the reasons for which the inhabitants were punished by the court were peculiar to the times, however some offences have familiar aspects and modern day equivalents. At the root of it all was the desire of those who were in positions of power and influence to assert a degree of order and control. After 1716 the orders made by the court, and presentments made to the jury, disappear from the court rolls. It could be argued that this when the power and influence of the manorial lord and his representatives began to wane. The establishment of petty sessions courts in the first half of the 18th century relieved the local manor courts of their responsibilities in dealing with minor offences, and power shifted to a different arena. But the exercise of that power was still rooted within the class system, as the people who became magistrates and justices of the peace in the new courts were the same individuals of wealth and influence who would have sat on the juries of the old manorial courts.

The court rolls of the manor of Childwall do not appear to exist after 1715, while the court rolls of Little Woolton under Lord Salisbury have survived into the 20th century and as late as 1940. However, the court persisted in this latter period merely as a means by which the sale, transfer and tenancy of land could be administered. Eventually the manorial lands in Little Woolton and Childwall were relinquished by Salisbury, and were acquired by the Liverpool Corporation, or divided up and sold to other private individuals or organisations, rendering the need for a manor court redundant.

THE OLD INNS OF
LITTLE WOOLTON AND CHILDWALL

Evidence of taverns or 'alehouses' in Little Woolton can be found as far back as the 1550s, and in Childwall the early 1600s. Records specific to licensing in this period are, at best, fragmentary, and this is in no small part due to the inconsistent state of regulation across the country around this time. Attempts had been made to regulate the brewing trade since medieval times, though this was mostly at a local level. The Alehouse Act of 1551 was passed in an attempt at the nationwide regulation of brewers and alehouse keepers, and was aimed at preventing the 'abuses and disorders' associated with the running of alehouses and tippling houses. Prospective alehouse keepers were required to be licensed and had to enter into a bond or 'recognizance' to ensure that they kept their establishments in good order. The earliest surviving alehouse recognizances for the parish of Childwall date back to 1620. An entry in the recognizance rolls for that year reveals the conditions under which licences were granted to the keepers of alehouses. It states:

'*The condition of this recognizance is such that whereas the above bonnde* (the name of the licensee appears here) *is admitted and allowed by the said justices to keepe a common alehouse or victualling house until the first day of May next ensuing the date hereof and no longer in the house wherein he now dwelleth at* (the town or village is recorded here) *in the said county of Lancaster and not elsewhere in the same county. If therefore the said* (name) *shall not during the time aforesaid permitte or suffer or have any playinge at dice card tables loggette bowls or any other unlawfull game or games in his house yard garden or backside, nor shall suffer to be or remain in his house any person or persons (not being his ordinary household servant) upon any Sabbath or holy day during the time of divine service or sermon, nor shall suffer any person to lodge or stay in his house above one day and one night but such whose true name and surname he shall deliver to some of the constables or in his absence to some of the officers of the same parish the next day following, unless they be such person or persons as he or she very well knoweth and will answere for his or theyr forthcominge, nor suffer any person to remaine in his or theyr house tipling or drinking contrary to the law, nor yet to be there tipling or drinking after niene of the clock in the night tyme, nor buy or take to pawne any stolen goods nor willingly harbour in his said house or in his barnes stables or otherwhere any rogues vagabonds sturdy beggars masterless men or other notorious offenders whatsoever, nor suffer any person or persons to sell or utter any beere or ale or other victuall by deputation or color of his or her license; and also he shall keepe the true assize and measure in his potts bread or otherwise in his uttering of his ale beere and bread and the same beere and ale to sell by scalled measure and according to the assize and not otherwise and shall not utter nor sell any strong beere or strong ale above a penny a quart, and small beere or small ale above a halfpenny the quart, and so after the same rates, and also shall not utter nor willingly suffer to be uttered drunke taken or tipled any tobacco within his house shoppe cellar or other place thereunto belonging , that then this recognizance to be voyded of none effecte or els to stande and remayne in full force for the kinge.'*

Although written in 1620, the conditions had not changed much from the passing of the 1551 Act, and, although subject to some changes and adaptations, many of the above elements still apply to licensed premises today.

Despite the prescriptive nature of the conditions, enforcement of them was another matter and appears to have been rather ad hoc. In Little Woolton, the manorial court was responsible for granting alehouse licences, though there was no requirement for the issuing of licences to be recorded. On the occasions that lists of licensees were made they were incomplete and not wholly accurate. In the surviving recognizance rolls covering Childwall and Little Woolton from 1631 to 1633, for example, some active alehouse keepers, who were regularly fined by the manor court in relation to assize of ale offences, do not appear. This suggests a tendency towards poor record keeping, apathy on the part of alehouse keepers towards obtaining or renewing licences, and negligent enforcement by the powers that be. In the absence of an independent professional body such as the police, who later took on responsibility for licensing matters, enforcement in relation to alehouses was the remit of the local alefounders or elected constable. Being local residents appointed by the manor court, and who were sometimes licensed victuallers themselves, their inclination and disposition towards reporting their friends and neighbours for licensing offences could be called into question. Even when alehouse keepers were presented before the court for operating without a licence, fines were low, and there was no other consequence or significant sanction. In the case of the township of Childwall, the absence of a manorial court prior to the mid-17th century meant that alehouse keepers before this time were probably operating unlicensed and with virtual impunity.

Despite poor record keeping in relation to the issue of licences and recognizances, there is other information about alehouses and their keepers in the records of the Little Woolton and Childwall manorial courts. The Little Woolton court rolls of 1553 mention four alehouse keepers - Thomas Orme, William Orme, John Fletcher and William Sadler - who were all fined by the court for keeping unlawful gaming in their houses 'contrary to the statute'. The men were also fined for breaking the assize of bread and ale, and William Sadler was fined for keeping an alehouse without lawful authority. While the court does not specifically state the location of these alehouses, they will almost certainly have been on or near the main thoroughfares through the township, of which there were but few. From other entries in the rolls of 1553 it can be ascertained that the house of John Fletcher was on the 'Churchway', now called Grange Lane, and may have been the tavern later occupied by several generations of the Halewood family. In 1565 alehouse keepers are mentioned again when William Orme and William Sadler were presented for having broken the assize of bread and ale, and were fined 3d each.

In 1584, there were five alehouse keepers mentioned in the court rolls of Little Woolton. William Sadler is still plying his trade, and is fined for keeping unlawful gaming in his house, while George Orme, John Byrne and William Halewood are fined for the same offence. This is the first mention of the name Halewood in relation to keeping an inn or tavern, and it is a name which would become almost synonymous with licensing in Little Woolton over the centuries that followed.

In the late 16th and early 17th century there is a notable gap in the manorial records of

Little Woolton. When they recommence after 1616 there are a handful of alehouse keepers mentioned in the rolls of the manor court. The court papers contain details of individuals who regularly transgressed against the licensing laws, and who had been presented to the court and issued fines for their troubles. Alehouse keepers are presented time after time, year after year, for assize or gaming offences, yet despite this recidivism, there seemed to be no real consequence to them continually contravening the licensing laws. The manor court appeared to be quite happy levying and collecting fines, and the alehouse keepers quite happy to pay them. This rendered the fines tantamount to a tax, helping to fill the township's coffers, but was no real deterrent or impediment to the ability of licensees to carry on their trade or renew their licence.

One of the first 17th century alehouse keepers in Little Woolton to be mentioned is James Welling, who appears in the manor court rolls of 1617. The following year, three other alehouse keepers are mentioned – Thomas Nailler, William Halewood and Henrie Halewood – however, they appear only once in the court papers, so it is difficult to ascertain where their alehouses were located. Welling, on the other hand, turns up regularly until 1635, and during this period several clues appear to indicate where his house stood. The same applies to a number of the other notable Little Woolton alehouse keepers, and they will be examined in more detail in the chapters that follow. It is clear that throughout the first half of the 17th century, a number of small country alehouses were dotted along the rural highways of the township. Mostly situated on or near the main road through Little Woolton to Tarbock and Warrington, or on the Churchway (Grange Lane), they would endure for a period of time, sometimes a couple of decades, sometimes less, before being superseded by another alehouse nearby. There always seemed to be at least three or four operating at any one time. The 1630s in particular appear to have been a golden time for Little Woolton's country alehouses. A number of individuals appear in the court rolls in this period for licensing offences, though some are mentioned only once and where they lived is not stated. In 1633, for example, George Brookes, William Gill and John Harockse are fined for selling ale without a licence, while at the same time, James Welling, David Catton, John Harrison and Thomas Halewood were all running alehouses in the township. Also in the 1630s there is mention of a Bryan Poole, William Sadler and William Birchall, each of whom is mentioned in a different year, so were possibly keepers of the same one or two houses during a period of quick turnaround of licensees. And in 1642, John Mollineux – who possibly lived on or near the Grange estate – was fined for assize of ale and gaming offences, but appears in the rolls in this year only. This apparent free for all in the brewing and beer trade did not last, however, and began to change when national events began to play themselves out at a local level.

The Interregnum which followed the civil war and Cromwell's victory in 1649 brought about a period of Puritanism and the promotion of an austere religious lifestyle that spread around the country, the effects of which were felt even in Little Woolton. Although Parliament seized those lands which were owned by the Crown and the royalist nobility, many wealthy land owners were able to retain their estates. The main landowners of Little Woolton, Gilbert Ireland of the Lee and James Brettargh of the Holt saw the sense of siding with the victors and became staunch parliamentarians, with Brettargh in particular reputed to have been a zealous puritan. In the eyes of the establishment, the less than virtuous pastimes and temptations offered by the likes of alehouses were frowned upon. It could be argued that fewer of the residents of the area were frequenting the alehouses as they sought to conform within the prevailing religious climate. Less demand meant making a living from brewing and selling beer was more difficult. More importantly for Little Woolton, most of the township's alehouses sat on land owned by Brettargh and Ireland, and it is most likely this fact that saw them go out of business in the years following the Parliamentarian victory. By the 1650s, only Edward Webster's Skillington House, which sat on land owned by John Cooke, remained in business within Little Woolton. Henry Glover, and Ales Cockett of the Cockshed estate, briefly tried to rekindle the trade in 1655 and 1659 respectively, but they could not make it last. It was not until after the restoration in 1660 that the licensing trade began to pick up again in Little Woolton, as the austere mood relaxed. Even the puritanical James Brettargh, whose forebears had always been royalists, underwent a complete sea change and became a noted tippler.

In contrast to the ebb and flow of alehouse numbers in Little Woolton, Childwall's three inns or taverns, all within striking distance of the church and market, retained a degree of stability during this period. For three inns or alehouses to remain viable in such a small and sparsely populated township may seem surprising, but there were a number of factors that contributed to their endurance and success.

From medieval times and before, Childwall had provided an important link between southern England and the North West. In this period, the River Mersey could be crossed at two ferry points, one in Liverpool and the other in Widnes. The only bridging point for people travelling up from the south was at Warrington, and, due to the topography of the area, Childwall was on the natural route to and from the region. Also, the sandstone ridge upon which Childwall sat provided a secure route to Hale, where travellers on foot or horseback could attempt to cross the Mersey by a rather hazardous and unpredictable ford. Childwall's location would have seen it receive numerous travellers over the years, and, during the English Civil War, significant numbers of soldiers making the journey to and from Liverpool, Hale or Warrington. Childwall would have been a relatively busy place, and there would undoubtedly have been plenty of business for its taverns in providing rest and refreshment to wayfarers.

Secondly, Childwall church was the main church for a parish which incorporated ten townships. Although each township eventually acquired their own churches or chapels of ease, the church in Childwall was, for many centuries, the main focus in the parish for weddings, baptisms and burials. There would have been ceremonies of one type or another taking place in the small village on an almost daily basis. In the 16th and 17th centuries it was common practice for funerals to be attended not just by friends and family, but by other members of the community, with every household expected send at least one representative. A funeral could be attended by eighty to a hundred mourners, and just as today, they would seek out food and drink afterwards. There would have been a similar demand generated by weddings and baptisms, and Childwall's alehouses near the church were ideally placed.

Thirdly, the centre of old Childwall was the location of the market which served Childwall, Little Woolton and possibly other nearby townships as well. In fact, one of Childwall's old taverns had the market on its doorstep. The market, which is mentioned in the manorial rolls of 1659 and 1665, was held on an area of open common land opposite the church. This land was eventually enclosed in 1813 and allocated to the vicarage. By this time the market had long ceased to be and the land became part of the grounds of the rectory. When in full operation, however, the market would have brought plenty of business to the three Childwall inns.

In 1659, when the Childwall manor court was revived, the three licensed houses of Childwall were going strong, with Edmund Wainwright, Gilbert Tarleton and William Marsh all in business. Their location at the hub of the parish certainly helped them through the interregnum, but there was also the fact that Childwall and its inns were in a period of instability in terms of ownership. Most of the land, including where the alehouses stood, had been owned by the Earl of Derby and had been seized by Parliament. As arrangements were being made, and deals being brokered for the sale of the manor over the decade that followed, life continued as normal in the township and the three inns remained in business. And so it was that Childwall boasted three inns or taverns until well into the 18th century.

After the restoration of the monarchy in 1660 the licensing trade in Little Woolton never quite recovered to the levels it had been at in the late 16th and first half of the 17th centuries. In 1666, Henry Halewood and John Parr appear as alehouse keepers in Little Woolton alongside Edmund Webster, though Parr only appears that year. For the remainder of the century there were only two alehouses in Little Woolton, compared to the three in Childwall.

As the 18th century dawned across the two townships, the nature of licensing began to change. The small rural alehouses from the Tudor and Stuart eras that had flourished in Little Woolton began to drift into obsolescence, eventually being succeeded by inns more suited to the changing demands of the times. The 18th century saw improvements in road building, advances in transport technology, and more relaxed regulations on the transport of goods by merchants. This led to an increase in traffic between towns and villages. No longer did inns and taverns just have to cater for locals or the occasional weary traveller, but also merchants and groups of coach passengers, along with their vehicles and horses. As a consequence inns needed to be bigger and have better stabling facilities and so the old houses were either modified into, or superseded by the larger inns. This period saw the establishment of several new inns in Little Woolton. The age of the smaller, older country alehouses in the area had come to an end.

As well as changes in the licensed houses themselves, new licensing laws came into effect around this time. For many years the authorities had found keeping track of alehouse licences problematic due to disorganised and inconsistent administration around the country. The difficulty in ascertaining who was licensed and who was not made it hard to prosecute alehouse keepers for certain offences, such as selling liquor without a licence. The Alehouses Act of 1753 was passed to bring some order to the situation. The Act decreed that alehouse licences would be issued on the same day each year at a special court held for the purpose. The recognizances were to be retained by the clerk of peace, and an accurate and complete register of all alehouse recognizances was to be kept. From this year onwards, the inn and alehouse keepers for each township can be identified, though the names of their establishments were not recorded until 1773.

In 1753, five licensed alehouse keepers are recorded in Little Woolton and Gateacre. These were William Davies of the Bear and Ragged Staff, David Edwardson of the Black Bull, Rosamund Finch, Henry Halewood of the Talbot and John Shaw. Shaw appears in this year only, and isn't licensed thereafter, so the location of his house is difficult to determine. The other four licensed houses of Little Woolton were all established in the first half of the 18th century, were of good size, and were ideally placed on main thoroughfares. In the same recognizance rolls, the keepers of Childwall's three, long established licensed houses are also recorded. There was Thomas Mather who ran the Abbey, Nathaniel Ashton of the Well Lane Inn, and Christopher Heyes of the inn at the market place. Rather than the inn keepers in Childwall and Little Woolton being in direct competition, there appears to have existed a spirit of cooperation between them, as they often stood as recognizance for each other at the licence renewal sessions.

By 1766 only the Abbey remained of the Childwall inns, while in Little Woolton and Gateacre the Black Bull, Bear and Ragged Staff and the Talbot survived. By the early 1800s, the Talbot, which had latterly been called the Dog, was also gone, leaving the two townships with only three inns between them. This was to remain the situation until the Beer House Act of 1830 which resulted in Little Woolton acquiring several beer houses and a new brewery on Gateacre Brow. The Gateacre Brewery was established to capitalise on the increased demand for beer that the new beer houses would create. In 1866, the final Victorian addition to the district's licensed houses arrived when the fully licensed house that would become the original Bridge Inn on Belle Vale Road was established. And so the number of inns and beer houses of Little Woolton and Childwall remained the same until the early 1900s, when new licensing laws instigated a cull of beer houses around the country. In nearby Woolton dozens of beer houses were closed, but Gateacre, which could boast just a handful of licensed houses, lost only Mercer's Railway Inn. The Halfway House beer house on Belle Vale Road would survive a little while longer, though it was eventually closed in 1938.

The Bear and Staff, Black Bull, Childwall Abbey, and former beer house the Brown Cow, are all still in business today, with the Bridge Inn having closed fairly recently. These old licensed houses have even outlived the host of modern public houses, which were built to service the new housing estates in the mid-20th century, and all of which, apart from the Childwall Fiveways, are now gone.

In order to better appreciate the history of the old houses, an examination of a couple of aspects of licensing law may be useful. A look at the Beer House Act of 1830 outlines the circumstances that led to the opening of the beer houses, and an explanation of the notion of the 'Bonafide Traveller' provides an overview of an aspect of licensing law that featured often in accounts of the public houses of the Victorian era.

THE BEER HOUSE ACT OF 1830

The Alehouses Act of 1828 did away with the recognizances and sureties that had been a requirement to obtain a liquor licence for over two centuries. A full licence was still required for inn keepers and victuallers to sell beers, wines and spirits, and these were granted by a special licensing court. Although recognizances were no longer needed, other conditions still had to be satisfied, such as the suitability of the premises and the prospective licensee. The Beer House Act of 1830, however, was a watershed in terms of licensing and public houses.

For many years the easy access to gin and its excessive consumption, especially amongst the lower classes, was regarded by the Establishment as a blight on society. Beer was seen as far less harmful, and a plan was formulated to make beer more accessible to the masses in order to offset the evils of gin. The Beer House Act of 1830 was passed by Parliament in an attempt to achieve just that. It was tantamount to deregulation of the retail sale of beer and cider, and allowed anyone to obtain, for a small fee, a beer licence from the local excise office. No real consideration was given to the suitability of the prospective licence holder or their premises. Although the holder of a beer licence was not allowed to sell wines or spirits, once the licence was obtained they were subject to the same laws as fully licenced houses in terms of conduct, opening hours and weights and measures.

The act resulted in an explosion in the number of the newly termed 'beer houses' around the country. In the village of Woolton, which had undergone a rapid population increase around the same time due in large part to the expansion of the quarry, the number of licenced houses rose from just one public house prior to 1830, to over 40 by 1870, with most of them being beer houses[1]. Little Woolton and Childwall did not undergo the same population explosion, so the impact of the 1830 Act was more modest. Still, a handful of new beer houses were established, those being the Brown Cow, John Blackburn's, the Folly Vale Tavern and the Halfway House on Belle Vale Road. As well as opportunities for licensees, the Beer House Act arguably precipitated the advent of the large commercial breweries, and companies such as Greenall's of St. Helens and Walkers of Warrington began to buy or lease great numbers of beer houses as outlets for their ales, becoming very successful as a result. The timing of the building of the Gateacre Brewery by John Fleetwood in 1830 was no coincidence, rather it was the recognition of the zeitgeist and the seizing of an opportunity to gain a foothold in a very profitable market.

The scale of the proliferation of beer houses around the country following the Beer House Act had been unforeseen by the government. A great many of the beer houses were small, unhygienic, and would have been considered wholly unsuitable had their owners applied to the court for a full licence. There were many opponents of the beer houses, including the church, police and various large employers, who claimed that the number of licensed houses was excessive and were causing the moral and physical decline of the population and in particular the poorer working classes. This resulted in the government spending the late 19th and early 20th century trying to undo the chaos that many had accused them of creating. Pressure was brought to bear on Parliament and several new acts were passed to try and reduce the number of licences, and to inhibit the number of new licences issued.

In terms of the courts and the enforcement of the licensing laws, the houses of Childwall and Little Woolton, like those in Much Woolton, came under the remit of the Woolton police and court. The changes in legislation that impacted the licensed houses of Woolton also affected those in Gateacre and Belle Vale, and at the turn of the 20th century they came under increased scrutiny. In 1903, before they issued the annual liquor licence renewals, the Woolton magistrates conducted personal inspections of the all licensed houses that fell within their remit. Most of the Gateacre houses, significantly fewer in number than their Woolton counterparts, were found to be deficient in some way, and were required to undergo improvements as a condition of their licence renewals.

A further Licensing Act in 1904 allowed the courts to close down pubs they saw as inadequate or superfluous to the needs of the community, with compensation being paid to owners and licensees. The Little Woolton houses fared somewhat better than those in Much Woolton. Of course there were a lot fewer of them to close, and it cannot be ignored that the most of the licensed houses in Gateacre were owned by William Hall Walker, son of Andrew Barclay Walker of the well-known brewing family. Colonel Walker was a local resident of some standing and a local MP. The Walker family had done much to improve the local village over the years, and held considerable influence. It is no surprise then that aside from the fully licensed houses, which always stood a better chance of survival, the Brown Cow and Halfway House beer houses, both owned by Walker, did not fall victim to the cull of the early 20th century. In contrast, the nearby Railway Inn on Belle Vale Rd, privately owned and leased to the Knotty Ash Brewery, was closed down due to being redundant in the area. The Walker's Brewery pubs in Woolton, such as the Cobden, the Coach and Horses and the Grapes, also survived, while swathes of houses belonging to other owners, for example Greenall Whitley, were closed down.

Eventually, by the early 20th century, the era of the beer house was more or less over. Many did survive, and most of the small, street corner Victorian pubs that are a still familiar sight today started their lives as beer houses. But many more have gone. In Woolton, only four former beer houses are still in business, while in Gateacre only the Brown Cow survives.

THE BONAFIDE TRAVELLER ISSUE

Of all the aspects of the licensing laws which brought the police and courts into conflict with licensees and their customers, the 'bonafide traveller issue' was a recurring and contentious one.

Prior to the 1840s the hours during which a licensed house could be open for business were more or less unregulated by the state, except for the general requirement for alehouses to be closed on Sundays during church services. Different areas often had their own ideas about what constituted reasonable opening hours, and there would be much variance from area to area. An act in 1839 which required licensed houses in London to close on Sunday mornings was extended to the rest of the country in 1842. Public houses had to close from midnight Saturday night until noon on Sunday. A further Act in 1853 required that licensed houses close at 11pm every night, and were not permitted to reopen until 4am. In 1854 and 1855, further adjustments were made to Sunday hours, with pubs only being allowed to trade between 1pm and 3pm, and 5pm and 11pm. The 1854 Act, amended and modified by later acts, allowed for exceptions to the prohibition of sale of alcohol outside of permitted hours in the case of 'bonafide travellers', a concept which was the subject of much legal debate and dispute in the magistrates courts. The idea of the act was to allow travellers engaged in long journeys to obtain alcoholic refreshment at a licensed premises outside of permitted hours should they develop a thirst. The act stated that a person would not be deemed to be a bonafide traveller unless the place where they had slept the previous night was at least three miles from the place where they demanded to be served with beer. The distance was to be calculated via the nearest public thoroughfare.

However, like many laws and regulations, there were always those who tried to use the law to their advantage. They would simply walk to a beer house or inn over three miles away, and claim this made them a traveller. Alternatively, they would tell a licensee, or the police if they called, that they had made such a journey, when in actual fact they were from somewhere much closer. Sometimes the police were able to prove that such a journey had not taken place, perhaps because they knew the drinker lived nearby, or the journey was measured to have been less than three miles. If it was found that three miles or more had been travelled, then this often resulted in no action being taken by the police and courts.

As tackling drunkenness became a major concern for the authorities in the late 19th century, the notion of the 'bona fide traveller' became more contentious. The courts found themselves under an obligation to take into consideration the nature of the journey, rather than just distance travelled. It was increasingly argued that those travelling to a public house three miles distant for the *sole purpose* of obtaining a drink outside of permitted hours would not be considered 'bona fide'. Such circumstances were said not to be 'in the spirit' of the act.

Of course, this did not stop people who were desperate to obtain liquor outside of hours from trying to use the three mile technicality to circumvent the licensing laws. Attempting to use the 'traveller trick' seems to have been a frequent practice for some hardened drinkers who couldn't go without beer on a Sunday afternoon. Court cases were fairly frequent, and a number of instances feature in the tales of the Gateacre houses which appear in this book.

Notes.

[1] *For more information see the author's 2018 book 'The Old Inns, Taverns and Beer Houses of Woolton'.*

CHILDWALL'S
THREE OLD INNS

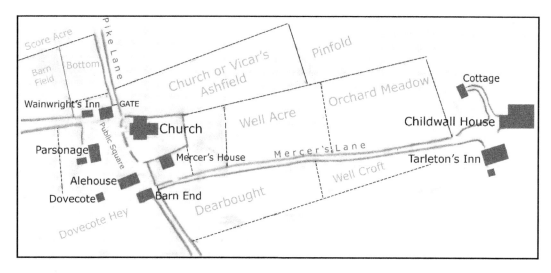

(Fig.16) Map showing the layout of the centre of Childwall township c1670, and the location of the three inns. The 'public square' was an area of common land where the market was held and where the stocks or pillory would have been located

WAINWRIGHT'S /
THE ABBEY

(Fig.17) The Childwall Abbey in around 1905

The Childwall Abbey can lay claim to be one of the oldest, if not *the* oldest, licensed house still in business in the district. As an inn or public house, it is older than the Black Bull and Bear and Staff in Gateacre, and possibly the Coffee House in Woolton Village.

There is no evidence that an abbey ever stood on the site of the Childwall Abbey Hotel. There are plenty of early references to Childwall Church, but none regarding an abbey. Archaeological excavations conducted at the Abbey Hotel in 1989 failed to find any indication that an abbey ever stood there.

Exactly when the first building was erected on the site is not clear, but a house stood there as far back as 1615, as this was the year that the 'messuage' and associated land was granted via indenture by William Earl of Derby to William Wainwright and his wife Alice at a yearly rent of three shillings and six pence. There is no record of it being an inn or alehouse at this time, though it may well have been. If it wasn't, it became one soon after. There is an indication that Wainwright may have rebuilt the earlier house into a more substantial building in around 1621, and there are still traces of this building within the current Childwall Abbey.

Although there are no records of the Childwall manorial court prior to 1659, the Wainwrights do appear in the rolls of the Little Woolton court. In 1638, a man called Richard Pendleton was fined 3 shillings and 4 pence by the court for taking heath from Little Woolton Hill and selling it to Wainwright's wife. In 1641, Edmund Wainwright (the son of William and his successor as tenant of his house opposite the church) acquired the lease for a small alehouse in Little Woolton which was occupied by Henry Leatherbarrow. This indicates that Wainwright was by this time involved in the licensing trade, perhaps having followed in his father's footsteps.

In 1652, 45 year old Edmund Wainwright and his wife Frances, still held the lease which had originally been issued to his father. His house, clearly an inn or alehouse by this time, is described as a messuage with brew house, kiln house, barn, stable, shippon, hemp yard and orchard. Wainwright also rented five acres of nearby land. It can be ascertained from the descriptions and information given that Wainwright's inn had not yet been enlarged into the grander Childwall Abbey that we know today.

In 1659, the Childwall manorial court, which had not been held for three decades, was revived by the new Lord of the Manor, Peter Legay. The innkeepers and alehouse-keepers of the township, who had operated unchecked during the court's lengthy hiatus, began to come under the scrutiny of the newly elected Childwall aletasters. The first Childwall innkeeper to be summonsed before the manor court that year was Edmund Wainwright, when he was fined for breaking the assize of bread and ale.

In 1661, Wainwright was ordered by the manorial court to make a gate at the end of his house across the entrance to the Pyke Lane, which is modern day Score Lane. He was also ordered to maintain this gate, and to keep in good repair the wall which ran from the gate along the Church Ashfield, a piece of land opposite the inn which was also leased by Wainwright. At court the following year, Wainwright was fined for breaking the assize of bread and ale, but was also found not to have maintained the wall as ordered and was fined ten shillings accordingly. Wainwright was fined for breaking the assize of bread and ale again in 1666. Records of the hearth tax in Childwall from that year reveal that Wainwright's inn opposite the church had no more than two hearths, another indication that it was a smaller inn rebuilt or enlarged at a later date into the structure we see today.

On the 25th October 1667 Edmund Wainwright was again fined by the manor court for breaking his assize of bread and ale, this time the sum of 12 pence. However in the following March[1] Wainwright died and his wife Frances took over the running of the inn.

Frances Wainwright appeared to fare no better than her late husband in avoiding the sanction of the manor court. Each year from 1668 to 1671 she was presented and fined for breaking the assize of bread and ale. After this, she seems then to have escaped prosecution for a number of years until, in 1679, Frances was fined by the court for breaking the assize of bread only, her measures of ale being in order.

Frances kept her inn until 1682, when 45 year old Joseph Longworth was granted the lease by Isaac Legay. Longworth's lease was for the inn and the Church Ashfield opposite, and the rental was 7 shillings, plus one day's reaping and one day's making of hay yearly. The inn is described as a building of three bays[2], with a garden and out buildings. Longworth became tenant of the inn along with his wife Sarah and took over the licence.

Almost immediately Longworth fell foul of the licensing laws and at the Manor Court held on 20th October, he was fined 1 shilling for breaking the assize of bread and ale. In 1683 Longworth is again fined by the court for *breakinge the assize of Beere*, yet at the same court he was elected to the role of constable for Childwall for the coming year. Perhaps not surprisingly, he does not appear before the court for any licensing breaches at the courts held in 1684. However, by 1685 he was before the court again for breaking the assize of ale and was fined 1 shilling (approximately £6 modern value). Longworth was regularly presented to the court and fined for assize offences, however in 1695 he was presented to the manorial court for a different offence. That year, the hill lookers of Little Woolton presented him for '*careying hether and gorse from Little Woolton Hill to Childwall*' and he was fined 6s and 8d. Just for good measure, or perhaps not, he was fined one shilling for breaking the assize of ale as well.

Longworth was the licensee of the inn for the rest of the 17th century. He was an active member of the manorial court, holding several different positions over the years, including constable, leylayer, and supervisor of the highways. After a number of years without being fined for assize offences, he found himself fined by the court every year from 1694 to 1699. From 1700 presentments of the alehouse keepers and innkeepers of Childwall stopped, which indicates that either they had become unfalteringly law abiding, or the aletasters had become less inclined to carry out their duties to the full extent. In a survey of Childwall in 1701 Longworth's inn is referred to as 'Wainwright's', and is still a building of only three bays. Joseph Longworth continued as the licensee of the inn until his death in 1711. For a short time his widow Sarah took over, but before long the inn was being run by Ellinor Abbot who was the daughter of Little Woolton inn keeper Henry Halewood. Ellinor had been married to George Abbot, but was widowed in 1711. Being from a long line of Little Woolton inn keepers, Ellinor would have been well versed in the brewing and licensing trade, and was an ideal candidate for taking over the Childwall inn. In 1714 and 1715, following the separation of the Childwall manor court from that of Little Woolton, the Childwall court was held at the house of Ellinor Abbot[3]. The court steward at the time was Isaac Greene, who resided at nearby Childwall House and was very soon to become lord of the manor.

After the early 1700s, the records of the Childwall manor court peter out, and do not survive at all after 1716. It is therefore unclear as to how long Ellinor Abbot was licensee of the inn, or who took over next, but she may have been at the inn long enough for it to be renamed after her. Was it at this time that Abbot's house became the Abbey? By 1747 the inn was occupied and run by Thomas Pigot, and his tenancy included the Church Ashfield opposite, sometimes referred to in later times as the Bloody Acre, and the land at the rear of the inn called the Barn Field. By this time the bowling green which sat next to the inn was in existence, though there is an indication that the green was for the use of the whole community rather than just patrons of the inn. The green was rented from the Lord of the Manor not by Pigot, but by Thomas Mather who occupied and ran an inn near to the ancient market place. Mather paid lord of the manor Isaac Greene 15 shillings a year rent for the bowling green.

By 1753, Thomas Pigot had left the Abbey and Thomas Mather had taken over, having moved from one inn to another. Mather was licensee of the Abbey until replaced by Robert Johnson in 1758. Johnson was himself replaced in 1770 by Francis Huxley, who had formerly been licensee of the inn that became the Coffee House in Woolton. In the alehouse recognizance records of 1773, the names of the inns in the area are recorded for the first time. Francis Huxley's inn is shown as the Abbey, which is the first time the name of the inn is recorded since being referred to as 'Wainwrights' over 70 years earlier. Huxley was licensee until 1776, when John Bibby was to become the new tenant.

John Bibby was at the Abbey for seven years, and was replaced in 1783 by Thomas Senar. Senar spent a decade at the inn, until William and Ellen Jackson became occupants of the

Abbey in 1793. William Jackson was the licensee until his death in August 1822. After Jackson's death, his widow Ellen took over the licence, but was to die just over a year later in September 1823. In October that year her son, William Jackson junior, applied to the Justices of the Prescot Division to take over the licence. Jackson was supported in his application by Henry Law who was the minister of Childwall Church, the churchwardens, the overseers of the poor, and several local inhabitants. A letter was written, signed by those several parties, in which Jackson was described as being '*a person of good fame, sober life and conversation, and a fit and proper person to be entrusted with a licence to keep an alehouse or victualling house.*' The application was successful, and Jackson ran the Abbey until his death at the relatively young age of 39 years on 22nd January 1830. William Jackson's sister Margaret ran the Abbey during the following year, but by 1831 the inn was in new hands. The successor to the Jacksons was 55 year old Robert Rimmer. The name Rimmer was to become synonymous with the Childwall Abbey, and the family were to have a long association with the inn lasting into the 20th century.

Robert Rimmer was licensee of the Abbey until he died on Sunday 10th March 1839 aged 64 years, and the licence passed to his widow Elizabeth. Elizabeth Rimmer ran the Abbey for a further 6 years before dying in 1845 aged 77. Her son Robert Rimmer junior then became licensee, and he ran the inn with his wife Jane. It was during this period of the Rimmers' tenure that the Abbey became a hostelry of some repute, and the resort of persons of some note and fame at that time.

In 1846 American physician, traveller and writer John Spence called at the Abbey, whilst on a tour of England, and wrote an account of his visit. Although he laboured under the misapprehension that the building he visited had once been an actual abbey occupied by monks, he does provide a description of the inn at the time. Spence describes entering the inn via a door-way overgrown with ivy, and finding himself in a rustic room adorned with 'dim and ancient' paintings. The table had been laid with food which consisted of a large round loaf two feet wide by one foot thick, a block of cheese just as large, along with butter and a jug of cream. Although describing it as simple and primitive fare, he lauds the food for its quality and richness. Spence then writes about the Abbey's leaded windows, made up of numerous small panes of glass four inches by three inches in size. The glass, as well as the wooden window shutters, had been carved and scratched almost to disfigurement by previous visitors to the inn. Names, initials and other graffiti, had been etched into their surface with knives or other sharp objects over the course of many years.

In September 1856, Robert Rimmer died, and his widow Jane took over the licence, and ran the Abbey for many years afterwards. As well as running the hotel, Jane Rimmer kept pigs, which she reared on land at the rear of the premises. In December 1867 a pig bred by Jane was exhibited at the Liverpool Christmas Cattle Show and was highly commended. In 1888 however, her pigs were struck with swine fever and had to be destroyed.

The Childwall Abbey continued to grow in popularity, attracting guests of a certain standing in society. Dinners and functions were hosted for numerous local societies, boards of directors, and groups consisting of local M.P.s and decorated military officers. As well as the hotel side of the business, the Abbey had a tap room for local workers which was at the rear of the building. This provided a place for the consumption of beer which was separate from the other part of the premises and served to keep the different classes of clientele apart.

The provision of a tap room, while undoubtedly held to be a good idea, was not without its problems for the licensee. In April 1883, she was summonsed to court on a charge of permitting drunkenness at the Abbey. On that occasion the case was not proved, however in August 1886 she was in court again accused with serving beer in the tap room at 3pm on a Sunday. She was convicted of this offence and fined 10 shillings plus costs.

In January 1888, the Childwall Abbey received a particularly distinguished guest in the person of Robert Gascoyne-Cecil, who was the British Prime Minister, Lord Salisbury and Lord of the Manor of Childwall. Whilst on his way to a function in Liverpool, Cecil called at the inn to see its licensee, Jane Rimmer. It seems that in her younger years, she had acted as his nurse when he was an infant and had resided at the nearby Childwall Hall. His short visit to the inn caused quite a stir locally, and the visit appeared in a number of newspapers around the country.

In 1888, Charles Millward, a musician, composer and noted writer of pantomimes and comic opera in the Victorian era, wrote of his fondness for 'Rimmer's Childwall Abbey Hotel', and recalled a number of specific visits there. His first recollection was of when he was a young boy in the 1840s. He had walked with a school friend from Liverpool to Childwall to look for birds' nests. Having found none they made their way to the Abbey and gingerly entered the tap room where they pooled their resources, which amounted to sixpence, and purchased some bread and cheese for their lunch. He recalls that even then the name 'Rimmer' was above the tap room door.

Millward's second visit to the Childwall Abbey came some years later, in about 1861. At the time he was an officer in 80th Lancashire Rifle Volunteers, or 'Press Guard' as they were known. On the occasion in question he had taken a company of the men on one of their regular marches. Millward paraded the men on the bowling green of the Abbey, and then each man was served with a meat pie and a pint pot of ale. The tee-totallers amongst them were 'graciously permitted' by Millward to have ginger beer instead of liquor, though it is clear in the tone of his writing that he held such 'total abstainers' from drink with a degree of disdain.

Having been reacquainted with the Childwall Abbey, he paid a further visit later in 1861, this time with a handful of guests from the world of the theatre. They were all members of the cast of the play 'The Colleen Bawn' which was being staged at the Liverpool Amphitheatre. All famous Victorian actors, they are named by Millward as John Drew, Sam Emery, Henry Mellon and J.C.Cowper. Millward described the moment when the party arrived at the hotel and entered the parlour. Sam Emery, who had never been to the Abbey, saw a portrait hanging on the wall and exclaimed, "Good God! That is my father!" It transpires that Emery's father, who had also been an actor and was described by Millward as the best country dialect actor on the stage in his day, was a good friend of Robert Rimmer, former licensee and late husband of the current proprietor. Emery's father used to stay at the Abbey whenever he was in Liverpool, and Jane Rimmer was herself taken aback when she recognised the son of her late husband's old friend. Millward goes on to name many other eminent theatrical stars who frequented the Abbey over the years, and who he describes as having partaken of the 'oldest and choicest wines' that Rimmer kept in the well-stocked cellar.

Millward's final visit to the Childwall Abbey came in 1862, when he brought a dozen or so members of the Savage Club to the inn. The Savage Club was an exclusive gentlemen's club, formed in London, comprised of men connected with literature and the arts, of which Millward was a member. A dinner was held for members of the club at the Abbey where Jane Rimmer is reported as having provided 'a feast for the gods'. After the dinner, the party adjourned to the bowling green to entertain themselves, before bad weather drove them back indoors. However, it was not before Liverpool photographer William Keith of Lord Street had taken a photograph of the assembled 'Savages' on the Abbey's green.

On 23rd March 1892, Jane Rimmer died, and in June her daughter Jane Elizabeth Rimmer took over the licence. Jane was the third generation of Rimmers to run the Abbey since her grandfather had taken on the old inn in Georgian times. It did not prove to be wholly plain sailing.

On 1st December 1893, Jane Rimmer appeared before the Woolton magistrates on Quarry Street accused of serving intoxicating liquor and having her house open during prohibited hours. It arose from an occasion when, on Sunday 26th November, PC Hartley of the local constabulary visited the Abbey at 4.20 pm. Upon entering the premises he found five men in a room opening into the stable yard, and not visible from the front of the house. On the table and mantle shelf were two pint pots and a half of ale. Two of the men, named McDonough and McConnell claimed they were in the employ of the licensee, and that a pint and half of the beer was theirs. Of the other three men, one was named Waterman and was a blacksmith from Gateacre, about a mile away, the second was a cabman called Hitchmough from Wavertree, also about a mile away, and the third was a man called Bolton, who was from Earle Road just under three miles away, and who claimed the remaining pint of beer. The constable told the court he had measured the distance to Bolton's house using a twenty yard tape. Lawyer Mr Swift defended licensee Rimmer, and claimed that neither Waterman nor Hitchmough had been served drink. Hitchmough had just dropped a woman off at the inn, and was warming himself by the fire, while Waterman was in there for the same purpose. The two employees were entitled to take refreshment, not being customers, and Bolton had entered the inn via the stable door unbeknown to the licensee. The bench sought an undertaking from Rimmer that in future, during prohibited hours, the stable house door would be kept closed to prevent persons entering the inn undetected. Rimmer promised to do this and the case against her was dropped.

In May 1896, Jane Rimmer once again found herself in trouble with the law. On Sunday the 24th of that month, PC Richardson called at the Abbey at about 10am and found a man called Daniel Grimley, from Liverpool, in the tap room. The man was described by the officer as being 'in drink'. The licensee was not present, as she was ill, so PC Richardson alerted the barman, James McConnell, as to the condition of the man. McConnell claimed he had not served him any drink. The constable left the inn, only to return at about 10.55am to find Grimley hopelessly drunk. He was escorted outside, though he was unable to walk without assistance, and once outside collapsed against a wall. The officer tried to walk Grimley along the road, but the man became helpless and the officer had to put him in a shed in a field while he went for assistance. When he returned, PC Richardson found Grimley asleep in the shed and he was transported to Woolton Police Station. The Woolton Court heard the case on 5th June. Barman McConnell stated he had come on duty at the tap room at 10am on the day in question, but he had not served Grimley with any beer. However, a witness called by the prosecution stated they had seen Grimley enter the inn at about 10am and that he was walking steadily and appeared sober. The court found the case proven and Rimmer was fined 10 shillings plus costs for permitting drunkenness, as, despite not being present during the offence, it was deemed in law that she still had overall responsibility for the conduct of the house. The male Grimley was also fined 10 shillings for being drunk on licensed premises.

At the licensing sessions in August 1896, Police Superintendent Baxendale objected to the renewal of the licence for the Childwall Abbey. This was on the grounds of the offence for which the licensee had been fined in June. Lawyer Edwin Berry was representing Jane Rimmer and while he accepted the conviction, he stated there were mitigating factors. Whilst under the Licensing Act a licensee was responsible for the acts and omissions of her servants, the fact was that Jane Rimmer was not present that day due to illness. The conviction was therefore down to just such an omission, and could not be used as evidence against the character of the licensee herself. Since Rimmer had held the licence there had been no other convictions against her or stains on the reputation of the inn, which had always been well run over the 65 years or so that the family had been there. The court accepted Mr Berry's argument and renewed the licence.

At the licensing sessions in August 1899, Jane Rimmer once again found her licence renewal being objected to. On this occasion it was claimed by the police that the tap room of the inn could not be directly supervised by the licensee when she was in the hotel part of the premises. Because of this the police were asking the court to order the tap room to be closed. Mr Rigby Swift, lawyer for Jane Rimmer, stated that while the Childwall Abbey catered for many distinguished guests and visitors, there were a number of farm labourers, carters and others local to the area who the licensee was also obliged to cater for. It was for this purpose that the tap room was in existence, the Abbey being the only licensed house within a mile. Without the tap room, argued Mr Swift, it would be impossible for the hotel to remain in business. The hearing was adjourned for a month, and when the next hearing took place a quite detailed description was given of the Abbey at that time. The hotel was described as a first class business, catering for a higher class of clientele. There was no bar in the hotel part of the house, but there was a smoke room where visitors could order and consume drink if they so wished. Local working people were not permitted in the hotel for fear they would 'ruin the class of business' that the hotel did, so there had always been a taproom at the rear of the premises to cater for them. Alterations had been made to the hotel in 1875, and the original taproom had been incorporated into the kitchen. A new taproom had been constructed which was farther back, and it was this, the policed claimed, that rendered it difficult for the licensee to supervise. Mr Swift argued that while it was true that Jane Rimmer could not physically oversee the taproom from the hotel, when customers made an order for beer in the taproom the attendant had to enter the hotel with the money, and fetch the beer back to them. The licensee could supervise this aspect of the transaction at least, and could keep a constant check on how much liquor was being consumed. The bench decided that the supervision of the taproom was not adequate, and that efforts should be made to bring it under the direct control of the licensee. It was suggested that some alterations be carried out inside the Abbey to comply with the court's wishes, and the licence was renewed on this basis. The chairman of the bench made it very clear that the situation should be rectified forthwith and that it should not be necessary to bring the issue before the court again in future. It appears the problem was satisfactorily resolved, as it was never raised again.

In 1904, Jane Elizabeth Rimmer decided to retire from the licensing trade. Having never married, she moved with her widowed sister Ellen to Port St Mary in the Isle of Man. In August that year, Jane's brother, Robert Rimmer, was granted transfer of the licence. Robert was to be the last of the Rimmer family to run the inn, remaining in charge for less than three years. In April 1907 the licence was transferred to William Gilbert Woodhouse. The only stain on Woodhouse's tenure appears to have been on 18th June 1909, when he was fined 2s and 6d for using unlawful measures to serve liquor.

David Robertson was the next licensee of the Childwall Abbey, being granted the licence in February 1913. Robertson was a prominent member of the licensing trade, as well as a freemason. He had held licences in Birkenhead and Southport before moving to Childwall. While based in the Wirral he had been chair of the Licensed Victuallers' Association, as well as sitting on the local council. His term as licensee of the Abbey was short-lived, however. On 12th November 1914, Robertson died at the relatively young age of 54 years. He was buried at All Saints Church opposite the inn. Succeeding him as licence holder was his widow Esther. Esther Robinson ran the Abbey for over a decade, finally relinquishing the licence in 1927.

After 1927, the Childwall Abbey, still owned by the Marquess of Salisbury, entered a period of instability, being licensed and leased to several individuals within a short space of time. In August 1927 William Robert Wilson took over, and in July 1928 the licence was transferred to Marion Hastie. In 1930, Frank John Brindley was granted the lease and the licence. However, before the end of the year, Brindley had left, and the lease had been acquired by Ernest Dobson. On 13th January 1931, the new lessee applied for the licence for the Abbey, and the circumstances surrounding application caused quite a stir. Dobson, a farmer from Market Drayton, appeared at the Liverpool licensing session at Dale Street Magistrates Court. He stated his intention to give up his farm, and to live at the Childwall Abbey with his daughters. He also intended to employ a woman with experience in the licensing trade to run the business for him. When the clerk of the court asked if there was any person present who had an objection to Dobson's application, as was the practice, a man, described as tall and well built, stepped forward and said, "I have. I object on moral grounds." The man in question gave his name as Harry Thomas Hulse, a hotel keeper from Market Drayton. In short, Hulse alleged that Dobson was having an affair with his wife, and had helped her by financing a cruelty lawsuit against him. The cruelty case had collapsed, and they were now separated, but it was his wife that Dobson intended to take to Childwall with him to run the hotel. Dobson denied the affair, and stated it was purely on a professional basis that Mrs Hulse was to be employed to run the Abbey, assisted by Dobson's daughter. After a series of exchanges between Hulse, Dobson and his lawyer, the hearing was adjourned for a month. Hulse intended to employ his own lawyer to cross examine Dobson regarding the whole affair. At the adjourned hearing on 10th February, Hulse attended with his lawyer, but Dobson, clearly not wishing the situation to be subjected to such scrutiny, withdrew his application for the licence. Instead, a subsequent application was made by John Morgan, who was now in the employ of Dobson. Morgan's application was successful and he became the new licensee of the Abbey.

This was not the end of the saga, however, and by March 1933 the management of the Abbey had descended into something akin to chaos, with the police raising the matter at the licensing sessions. Their issue was not with licensee Morgan, but with the lease holder, Ernest Dobson. They argued that Morgan was not in control of the premises, as he should be, and was not allowed any say in the running of the Abbey by Dobson. Giving evidence to the court, Morgan confirmed this and stated that he was denied any autonomy by Dobson, and suffered constant interference from an acquaintance of Dobson's referred to as 'Mrs Hulse'. Mrs Hulse was a frequent visitor to the hotel and constantly meddled with how Morgan conducted the business. The police argued that the employment of Morgan by Dobson was merely a 'front', allowing Mrs Hulse to conduct the business behind the scenes. The police were not happy with this situation, and neither was Morgan, who had given his notice to quit. Dobson was now putting forward a new licensee to take over. This was Arthur Thomas Mitchell. The police had no issue with Mitchell, but had every issue with the lessee Dobson who they felt would not allow Mitchell to run the house without interference. Ultimately, the court agreed to transfer the licence to Mitchell to allow the business to stay open, but directed that Dobson take steps to surrender his lease, and that 'Mrs Hulse' desist from visiting the premises and interfering with the business. This was acceptable to the police, and to the Abbey's owner, Lord Salisbury, who had a representative in court. On 12th September 1933 the Childwall Abbey had a new lease holder in Doris Kathleen Gardner, who was also granted the licence. Gardner had previously been the licensee of the Oxford Hotel in Manchester.

During her tenure of the Abbey, Doris Gardner got married and became Doris Bloom. While continuing to hold the lease, she employed a licensee to run the inn for her, in the person of W.J. Sheil. In March 1939, the Liverpool licensing court received an application from Higson's brewery, who were proposing to build a new hotel at the Childwall Fiveways. Amongst the local residents who gathered to oppose the building of the new public house was Sheil, who was concerned that a new hotel would take business away from the Abbey. Although the onset of the Second World War delayed things somewhat, any opposition ultimately proved fruitless, and the new hotel at the Fiveways was eventually built. Despite those initial fears, the Childwall Abbey survived the establishment of the Childwall Fiveways pub and survives in business to this day. One of the oldest surviving inns in the Liverpool region, it is still a popular pub, eatery and hotel.

(Fig.18) The Childwall Abbey Hotel photographed from the tower of All Saints Church in 2019

Notes:

[1]This would still have been March 1667, as it is necessary to note that prior to 1752 England and Wales used the Julian calendar with the year commencing on 25th March and ending on 24th March 12 months later.

[2]A bay in this context is an architectural term meaning a distinct section of a structure, for example the front of a building having two windowed rooms either side of a main doorway could be seen as having three bays. By contrast the current Childwall Abbey is described as a building of nine bays.

[3]There are a number of cases of manor courts being held in inns or hostelries. In 1726, for example, the court for the manor of Sefton was held at an alehouse near to Sefton Church in Lunt, most likely the house currently known as the 'Punch Bowl'. Incidentally, Isaac Greene was involved in the stewardship of this manor court also.

DATING THE
CHILDWALL ABBEY

As there appears to be no record of the actual building of the inn, or when it was established, settling on a precise date for the origins of the Childwall Abbey can prove difficult. There are, however, clues which provide at least some insight as to its beginnings and long history.

(Fig.19) The 17th century ionic stone capital over the front door of the Abbey. Remnants of the greatly weathered design and what appears to be part of a date can just be made out. The '1' either side of the '6' and '2' are obscured by repairs.

Pevsner's Architectural Guide of Lancashire describes the Abbey as a 'late Georgian Gothic Inn' but draws attention to a 'primitive Ionic capital' over the front doorway of the premises. The worn stone plaque is described as late 16th or early 17th century type, and the guide questions how such a feature could have come to be on what appears to be a later building. After permission was granted by the Abbey, the feature has been subject to close scrutiny, and is indeed a heavily weathered and eroded sandstone capital. Unfortunately it has been clumsily and unsympathetically repaired in the past with blobs of cement or mortar, which has served to obscure some of the worn original carvings. However, close examination reveals traces of the old relief which once adorned the stone, certain details of which can still just be made out, though other details are probably permanently lost. As well as impressions of the carved scrolling down the sides of the capital, the numbers '6' and '2', in a font style typical of the 17th century, are faintly visible. This would indicate a date of 1621 or thereabouts. William Wainwright was granted a lease for the house in 1615 by the Earl of Derby, at a yearly rent of 3 shillings and 6 pence. The capital could suggest that Wainwright rebuilt or improved the original house in 1621. The front or central part of the current building could date from this time, or, as is more likely, the old stone was saved and incorporated into the structure when it was rebuilt into its current form. It would also suggest that Pevsner's Guide got the dating of the capital spot on and it is indeed an early 17th century feature which has been retained during later modifications.

(Fig.20) A suggested design of the date stone before centuries of weathering and repairs took their toll

We know there was a building on the site as early as 1615, in the 1660s it had no more than two hearths, and in 1701 it was still a building of only three 'bays' or sections. This is less than half the size of the current premises. In the Yates and Perry map of 1768, the Abbey appears as a more substantial structure, and this is around the time it became Childwall's only surviving inn. To assume this mantle, and to safely supersede the other two inns and handle the extra demand their absence would bring, would have required it to have adequate accommodation. The earliest renderings of the Abbey from around the early 1800s show it more or less as it appears today, minus, of course, the Victorian extension to the north side. Given all the evidence, it can be confidently argued that the Abbey arrived in its current form sometime in the period between 1701 and 1768.

So when and why did the inn become known as the Abbey? We know there was never an actual abbey at the location, the only religious building being the church opposite, which may have started life as a chapel dedicated to St Peter. When the inn was rebuilt or enlarged, great effort was made to make it resemble an old ecclesiastical building. The windows are of an ogee or pointed style popular in the medieval period and used extensively in church and religious buildings throughout the centuries. The stone heads over each of the building's windows also give the building a monastic appearance. Given the effort and expense involved in achieving such a look, it is unlikely to have been an accident. Why would so much effort be made to make an inn to look like an abbey if that was not already its name? There is a strong possibility that the inn was called the Abbey at the time it was enlarged, and was remodelled to reflect its name, rather than the other way around. Given that no account of the naming or rebuilding of the inn appears to exist, this may only ever be speculation. What is beyond doubt is that the inn was called the Abbey by 1773, when the names of inns and taverns of the area were named in the alehouse recognizances for the first time. The name undoubtedly predates this year, which opposes an idea propounded by some early 20th century historians and authors, such as F.H. Cheetham and Chris Healey, which has gained traction over the years. Their suggestion was that the inn was named after Bamber Gascoyne's rebuilt Childwall Hall, which was also known as Childwall Abbey. A number of articles printed in the Liverpool Daily Post and Echo newspapers in the 1930s reiterated and helped to propagate this notion. But Gascoyne's 'Abbey' was not built until 1780, seven years after the first record of the inn being called the Abbey.

(Fig.21) One of the Childwall Abbey's ogee headed windows topped with a stone face, a feature which was most likely dates from when the Abbey was rebuilt or enlarged in the Georgian period in the first half of the 18th century.

A strong contender for the origin of the name 'Abbey' is that in the first part of the 18th century the inn was run by licensee Ellinor Abbot. There is a long tradition of inns and alehouses being named after their keepers. Having been occupied for much of the 17th century by the Wainwright family, the inn was still referred to as Wainwright's even when under the tenure of Joseph Longworth. In 1714, it was referred to as the house of Ellinor Abbot. The institution run by an Abbot is an Abbey, so it a plausible theory that this is when and how the Childwall Abbey acquired its name.

THE WELL LANE INN

An old inn or tavern once stood at the bottom of Well Lane, near to Childwall House manor house. If this establishment had a name, which it most likely did, then it is currently lost to time, as there is no record of what it was called. Given its location on Well Lane, its close proximity to the Childwall well, and nearby tracts of land being known as the Well Croft and the Well Acre, it would be easy to imagine that it bore a name with a similar connotation, for example 'The Well Inn', however this is mere conjecture. The fact is, the inn on Well Lane had closed for business before 1773, when the names of the inns and taverns in the area were finally recorded in the alehouse recognizances of the West Derby Hundred, and so what it was called may never be known.

Exactly when the inn on Well Lane was first built is unclear, but there is record of it being granted at a rent of three shillings per year to Thomas Broughton in 1608 by William Earl of Derby. In 1652 when a survey of Childwall was conducted on behalf of Parliament, it was a substantial and well-established hostelry. It was still in the occupation of Thomas Broughton, who was by this time 73 years of age, and was described as consisting of a hall and two parlours, a kitchen, buttery, a cellar, a brewhouse and a malthouse, and six upper rooms. The inn also had a stable, shippon, dove house, garden, orchard, hemp yard and eight acres of associated lands.

By 1660 the inn had a new occupant and licensee in Gilbert Tarleton. That year he appeared in the manor rolls of Little Woolton and Childwall for not keeping the assize of bread and ale. Tarleton was regularly fined over the years that followed for assize offences. He also kept pigs, and was on several occasions fined for failing to comply with local livestock regulations. In 1662 he was fined one shilling for not yoking his swine, and in 1666 and 1675 was presented by the burleymen and fined by the court for not ringing his swine.

As well as an inn keeper and pig keeper, Tarleton was an active officer of the court, fulfilling numerous roles. In 1662 he was elected burleyman, aletaster, firelooker and 'appraiser of horses'. In 1665, Tarleton became tenant not only of the Well Lane inn, but of Childwall House itself. The same year he was elected a supervisor of the highway, and in 1668, Tarleton was elected constable for Childwall.

Gilbert Tarleton ran his inn until 1685, when Jennet Birch is shown as having taken over. Birch is presented before the court that year for breaking the assize of bread and ale. Birch appears only once in the rolls, and the next recorded tenant of the inn in Well Lane is Thomas Knowles.

Knowles appears as the licensee of the old inn in 1694, as under tenant to Mary Broughton who held Childwall House, the Well Lane inn and the attached estate. In 1695, Knowles is presented and fined for breaking the assize of ale, and then each year thereafter until 1699.

In 1705 William Whitfield took over the lease from the Broughton family. Thomas Knowles remained as tenant and licensee of the inn in Well Lane until at least 1715, when the records of the Childwall manor court cease.

By 1729, the tenant of the inn on Well Lane was Nathaniel Ashton and his wife Ellen. By the 1740s, the house and estate was in the possession of James Moffit, with the Ashton's as under tenants. Ashton was to be the final licensee of the Well Lane inn, In 1763 Ellen Ashton died, and Nathaniel gave up his licence and moved away.

After 1763, the inn is not shown as being licenced again. The old inn which had stood at the bottom of Well Lane, in the shadow of Childwall House, had ceased to be. How long it stood for after this date is unclear, but by 1780 Bamber Gascoyne, Lord of the Manor of Childwall, had demolished the old building and had built a new house – intended as a dower house[1] for his wife – on or near the site. This house and the attached land became known as Lower Farm. Lower Farm, along with Childwall House itself, are both gone and demolished, and built over with a modern housing estate. No traces of the old buildings remain.

[1] A dower house is a house built for a widow to live in following the death of her husband. The idea was that the widow would vacate the main family house, leaving it free for the next male heir to inhabit with his family.

THE MARKET PLACE INN

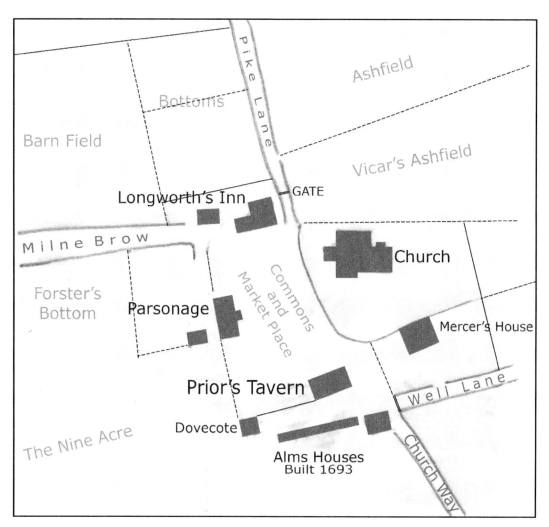

(Fig.22) Map showing the centre of Childwall c1700, and the location of the tavern ran at that time by Samuel Prior. Note Mercer's House, which was built against the Churchyard wall, and pre-dated the Georgian built Elm House which currently stands on the site.

Childwall's third ancient inn or tavern, the name of which is lost to time, stood opposite the entrance to Well Lane, near to the vicarage and market place. Later, after Isaac Greene had built his new Childwall Hall, the inn stood in its shadow. The old house had its own malt house for distilling whisky, but unlike the nearby Abbey, did not appear to have its own brew house. The house was in the possession of the church, and with the original vicarage having a brew house, it is likely that this is how the tavern was supplied with ale.

The first indication of the existence of the third inn in Childwall is in 1647 when Thomas

Sadler appears in the alehouse recognizances. In 1662, William Marsh appears both in the alehouse recognizances for Childwall, and in the manorial records for breaking the assize of bread and ale. Marsh appears regularly in the manorial records for assize of ale offences, until in 1670 he is replaced as licensee by Alice Chambers, who herself is fined by the manor court for breaking the assize of ale.

The next time the alehouse at the market place is mentioned is in the court rolls of 1683, when the then licensee Henry Woodbourne is presented for breaking assize of bread and ale, He is presented again in 1685.

In 1694, after the aletasters of Childwall had been admonished by the court for not bringing in presentments for several years, a new licensee of the market place alehouse is recorded. This is Samuel Prior, who was tenant to John Hunt on behalf of the trustees of the vicar of Childwall. In 1695 and 1696, Prior was presented to the court for breaking the assize of ale. In 1697, however, the Childwall aletasters were fined for failing to report Prior for assize offences.

Samuel Prior was presented for breaking the assize of ale up until 1699, after which presentments of the alehouse keepers of Little Woolton and Childwall suddenly cease. In 1706 the occupant and keeper of the alehouse was Robert Fletcher. Initially, Fletcher was an under tenant, but in 1711 he acquired the lease, becoming chief tenant of the property.

By 1747 the inn by the ancient market place was occupied by Thomas Mather, and referred to as late Fletcher's. Mather paid the Lord of the Manor £8 10s per year for the rental of the house, and he also held by lease several other parcels of land nearby. This included the bowling green and outhouse next to the Abbey, for which he paid 15 shillings per year. By 1753, Mather had moved to take over the Abbey, and Christopher Heyes took occupancy of his former inn.

Heyes ran the inn until 1765, after which the licence was allowed to lapse. The reason why the inn fell out of use, or why it was eventually demolished is not clear. It may just have been that it was an ancient building which had had its day. Whatever the reason, it had gone by the late 18th or early 19th century. The site became part of the vicarage grounds, and is now built over with the Childwall Abbey School.

WILLIAM TARLETON'S HOUSE OF THE BROOK CROFT

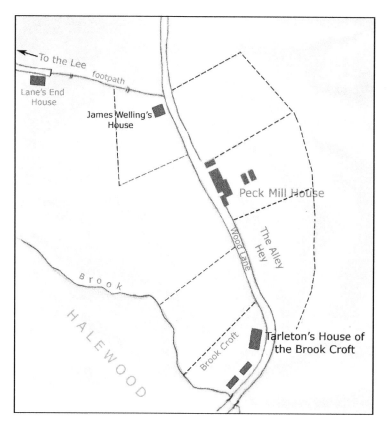

(Fig.23) Map showing the locations of the House of the Brook Croft and James Welling's alehouse in the 17th century. Almost opposite the Brook Croft is the Alley Hey which would have been near to William Brookes' bowling alley. Also shown is the original course of Wood Lane and Peck Mill House, both of which have been built over with a housing estate.

The House of the Brook Croft was an old alehouse which stood at the end of the old Wood Lane near to the border with Halewood.

In the late 16th and early 17th centuries, the house was held copyhold by Thomas Orme of the Lee estate. In 1620 it was held by Edward Fox, and was occupied by his under tenants who were William Tarleton and his wife Ann. Tarleton was a licensed victualler and kept the house as an alehouse. In the manorial court of May 1620, William Tarleton was presented before the court and fined 2 shillings for keeping unlawful gaming in the house. At the same court he was also fined 12 pence for having a fight, or '*tussell*', with a man called Randle Spencer, and in October the same year he was fined for breaking the assize of bread and ale.

Tarleton was fined again in 1622 for keeping unlawful gaming in his house, but apart from this offence, Tarleton kept a more orderly and well run house compared to many of his fellow inn keepers, and was presented for licensing offences less often.

In 1626 and 1627, William Tarleton was appointed as an officer of the Little Woolton Court, and, along with Thomas Leatherbarrow, was an aletaster for those years. The clear conflict of interest is an example of how open to abuse the manorial system was, and unsurprisingly Tarleton was not presented before the court for any misdemeanours during his tenure. In fact, Tarleton was not to appear before the Little Woolton manor court for licensing offences again. By 1633 William Tarleton had died, and his house was let to Ann Bane, the daughter of a local gentlemen called James Bane. Tarleton's alehouse licence died with him, and the house was not operated as such again.

By 1640, a number of new dwellings had been built on the land at the rear of Tarleton's old house, and several residents are recorded, including Anne Dobson, Henry Baxter and William Hartley.

William Tarleton's former alehouse on the Brook Croft had numerous occupants in the centuries that followed. Among them were William Knowles, John Bispham and in 1660 John Knowles, a tailor. The house was still referred to as Knowles House when it came into the occupancy of Peter Rishton and his son Robert in 1702. Eventually, having once been part of the Lee estate, the house and seven acres of adjoining land was absorbed into the Peckmill estate surrounding Peckmill House which was owned a succession of wealthy landowners such as the Reverend John Entwistle, Foster Cunliffe and Colonel George Williams.

(Fig.24) The original Wood Lane in modern day Netherley, which once hosted a number of Little Woolton's ancient rural alehouses. Now it leads into a modern housing estate, and a series of dead ends and footpaths.

The House of the Brook Croft is too old to have survived in anything near its original form, however there are houses on the site which are themselves of some age. Of all the once rural sites of the ancient alehouses, the area of land originally known as the Brook Croft is one that has seen the fewest changes since the earliest times. Until very recently the land was relatively undeveloped, with only a few centuries-old cottages and houses upon it. The brook from which it took its name still flows, forming a natural border between Netherley and Halewood, but the old Wood Lane has been built over, a new Wood Lane being established several hundred yards to the north. In 2019 development began on a block of modern apartments on the Brook Croft which will dwarf the old cottages and change the nature of the Brook Croft probably forever.

(Fig.25) An old cottage which stands on land once known as the Brook Croft on Wood Lane near the Halewood border. This cottage is several centuries old, and of a style consistent with the 17th century or earlier. It is entirely possible that this cottage dates back to around 1640 when several new tenants are recorded on the land. It appears to have been only moderately renovated over the years, and probably once had a thatched roof.

WILLIAM BROOKES' BOWLING ALLEY

Both the townships of Childwall and Little Woolton possessed a bowling alley in the 16th century. Childwall's bowling alley was on what is now Childwall Abbey Road, and had fallen out of use by the 17th century, eventually becoming part of Webster's Farm. A piece of land attached to the old bowling alley in Childwall was known as the Alley Hey, and retained this name as late as the 19th century, long after the bowling alley had ceased to be.

There was also an Alley Hey in Little Woolton, which would have been attached to or near the bowling alley, hence its name. The land was at the south end of the township, near to the border with Halewood, and was part of the Peck Mill House estate.

In the rolls of the manor court of 1584, an alehouse keeper is mentioned by the name of William Brookes. In the court records it states that '*William Brookes has kept and frequented illicit gaming in his house and kept bowling and a bowling alley and hath frequented bowling commonly.*' He is fined 3 shillings and 4 pence. Brookes was also fined for keeping illicit gaming the following year.

The Alley Hey was virtually opposite William Tarleton's House of the Brook Croft (see fig.23), and in the early 1600s was held by Tarleton as part of his tenancy. William Brookes' 16th century alehouse and bowling alley would have been around this location, and may have been part of Peck Mill House, or was perhaps the house which became William Tarleton's alehouse. Whichever it was, the alley had fallen out of use as such by the 17th century, and, like Peck Mill House and William Tarleton's house, is long gone.

JAMES WELLING'S RYDING

(Fig.26) The overlay shows the original course of Wood Lane before being built over in the 20th century, and the locations of (A) James Welling's house, (B) Peck Mill House and (C) William Tarleton's house of the Brook Croft. The brook is the natural border between Halewood and the old Little Woolton Township. Satellite view from Google Earth (c) Google Inc. 2020

One of Little Woolton's earliest recorded inn keepers, James Welling can be found in the rolls of the manor court from 1617. His alehouse was situated on the old Wood Lane, close to an ancient footpath or right of way leading into the grounds of the Lee. It was part of the Lee estate, but was owned copyhold by Richard Woodes, and was known as Woodes Ryding and later, Hunts Ryding.

One of the main concerns for the early manor court in relation to the old alehouses seems to have been unlawful gaming, an activity which contravened the conditions of an alehouse licence. The issue was fairly prevalent at the time, and in October 1617, innkeeper James Welling was presented to the manor court for permitting unlawful gaming in his house, as well as for gaming himself. He was fined 12 pence for each offence, while Henry Arnot and Thomas Hocksie were also fined for gaming.

In May 1620, Welling was fined 2 pence for selling ale without a licence, and in October that year he was fined 6 shillings 8 pence for not keeping the assize of bread and ale. The following year, 1621, he was again fined for selling ale without a licence, having been '*warned by the constables*', and was also found permitting unlawful gaming in his house.

In the May court of 1622, James Welling was fined for keeping unlawful gaming in his house at an inconvenient time. Those caught gaming were also fined, and they were James Halewood, Thomas Bridge, William Orme, and John Hocksie the younger, who all had to pay a fine of 6 pence each. James Halewood and Richard Halewood were also fined at the same court for gaming at Welling's house on another occasion. The wife of James Welling, Catherine, was fined 12 pence for *'lending monaye unto Richard Halewood to game in her house the said Richard Halewood being under age'*. Just to compound the gaming issue at Welling's alehouse, John Hocksie the elder, who was at that time Little Woolton's bailiff, was caught unlawfully gaming with James Welling when he should have been carrying out his duties and both he and Welling were fined. Hocksie was fined 12 pence, double the amount levied against Welling.

At the October court of 1622 Welling found himself in a fair bit of trouble at the manor court. He was fined for keeping a house of *'bodrie'*, meaning a bawdy or disorderly house. He was also fined for keeping unlawful gaming in his house, and for harbouring Randle Spencer and John Lalent *'being two tainted fellowes'*. For his troubles he was ordered by the court to cease keeping an alehouse within one week of the court session. It seems this stripping of his license was merely temporary, as by 1624 Welling reappears in the court records as an alehouse keeper. Again he was punished for keeping unlawful gaming in his house, and over the next few years was further fined for the recurring and predictable offence of failing to keep the assize of ale.

In 1629 Welling was fined by the court for *'not selling a quart of ale for a penny'*, and was before the court for not selling his ale in the correct quantity in 1630 and 1631. Also in October 1631, Welling was fined 9 shillings and 8 pence for permitting unlawful gaming in his house, as well as gaming himself at an unlawful time of the night. The other unlawful gamers, who were fined 3 shillings and 4 pence each, were John Cockett, Thomas Yeats from Tarbock, James Halewood and Thomas Halewood. It appears to have been quite a night at Welling's house that evening, as Yeats and Thomas Halewood were also fined for fighting, or *'makinge a tussle upon the bodie'* of each other. Welling was being fined for breaking the assize of ale annually at this point, though apart from a negligible fine there did not seem to be any real sanction.

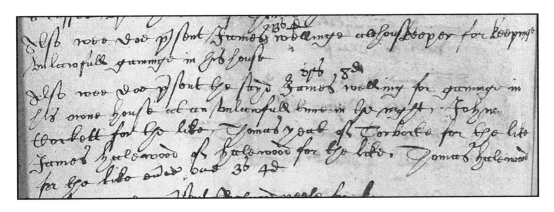

(Fig.27) Entry in the Little Woolton court rolls for 1631 which reveals unlawful gaming at James Welling's house, and the names of those involved. From the records of the Salisbury estate, used with permission of Liverpool Record Office, Liverpool Libraries.

In 1632, a man called John Harrison was fined 2s for *'burstinge open James Wellinge his house dore at an unconvenient time of the night'*. John Harrison is recorded as being a fellow alehouse keeper around this time, though it does not state what the purpose of this unwanted visitation was.

In 1634 the record of an assize offence committed by Welling contains some rare detail, when he was presented before the jury for '*selling ale by a quart which is but a pynt and a halff*', and was fined 3 shillings and 4 pence. In October the same year, the alehouse keeper was again before the court when he was fined 3 pence for '*not lodging a traveller who came to his house in sufficient time*'. At the same court, two men called Thomas Harrison and John Hill were fined by the court for abusing James Welling and his wife in their house.

James Welling is one of the few Little Woolton alehouse keepers who appears in the incomplete and ad hoc early 17th century alehouse recognizances for the parish of Childwall. He is recorded in 1630, 1634, when he also stands recognizance for fellow alehouse keeper David Catton, and in 1635.

By 1647 Welling had died, and his house and land passed to the occupation of Richard Woodes and became known as Woodes Ryding. The former alehouse of James Welling, which appears to have been quite a lively and colourful place, was not licensed again. Before the mid-19th century, Welling's old house had been demolished, leaving an area of pasture land which became part of John Okill's Lee estate. Since then the course of Wood Lane has been changed, and the old road and site of Welling's house have been built over by modern housing.

JOHN HARRISON

John Harrison was an alehouse keeper who was active in the 1630s. A contemporary of James Welling's, he appeared to be something of a rival also. In 1632, Harrison was fined by the court for '*burstinge open James Wellinge his house dore at an unconvenient time of the night*'. This would tend to suggest that Harrison lived somewhere near fellow alehouse keeper Welling on the old Wood Lane. The purpose of Harrison's visit is not stated, but it does not appear to have been a friendly act, and there may have been some kind of friction between them.

In 1634 John Harrison appears before the court for licensing offences when he is fined for selling ale without a licence. In April 1636 Harrison is fined 3s 4d for not keeping the assize of ale. In the October the same year he was again fined for assize offences, and an additional 3d for not turning up for court. By October 1637 Harrison had died, and it does not appear his widow Alice continued to run the house as an alehouse.

GEORGE BROOKES

George Brookes, also occasionally spelt 'Brooks', appeared in the Little Woolton records as early as 1624, when it is recorded that '*at the division of the commons within this manor there was eight yeards in brede lefte for a common lane betwixt George Brooks house and Thos Johnson's house without other stops or set of yeate or stile*'. Johnson was tenant of the Lee at this time, so this puts Brookes' house on the old Tarbock Road (later Belle Vale Road, and now Childwall Valley Road), near to the entrance lane leading Lee Manor (see fig.28). This lane, later gated by John Okill, is now the entrance and driveway to Lee Manor Golf Club.

Brookes' first appearance before the court for a licensing offence is in 1633, when he is presented for selling ale without a licence. Not having learned his lesson, it seems, Brookes is presented and fined by the court the following year for the same offence. In 1635, George Brookes escapes sanction, suggesting that he had acquired a licence for that year. However, in 1636 he is fined once again for '*selling beare without licence of the steward contrarie to a former order*'. He does not appear for licensing offences again, however in 1638 he is fined 12d for pulling down hedges belonging to the Lee estate. By 1640 George Brookes is shown as having died, and was survived by his wife Alice. One thing can be said for Brookes, and that is that he was never fined for assize offences, unlike most of his contemporaries. This obviously means he sold ale of good quality and in proper measures.

DAVID CATTON

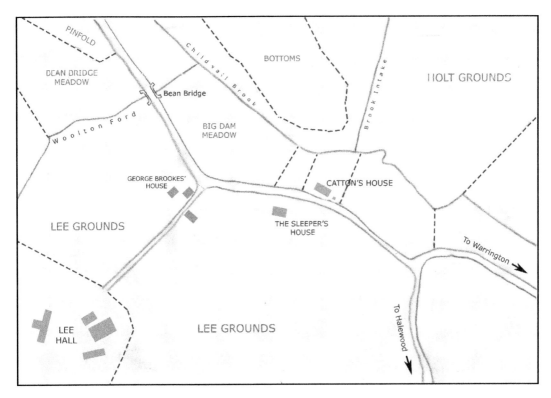

(Fig.28) Map showing the location of Catton's alehouse in the first half of the 17th century. Also shown is the location of George Brookes' alehouse and the 'new' lane of 1624 leading to the Lee Hall manor house.

Catton's alehouse stood on the old section of Belle Vale Road, just North West of where it split into Netherley Road and the original Wood Lane. Both the road and the site of the old house have been built over with a housing estate, and no trace of either remains.

David Catton was an alehouse keeper in Little Woolton between the years 1633 and about 1638, however he may have been preceded at his alehouse by Thomas Lightbourne, who is recorded as a licensee in the court rolls in 1631 and 1632. Catton first appears in the manor court records in April 1633 when he was fined 6 shillings and 8 pence for *'keeping ale to sell without licence'* and for keeping unlawful gaming in his house. He quickly rectified the former transgression, and the same month the granting of a licence to Catton is recorded in the alehouse recognizances. In October the same year he was fined for not keeping his assize of bread and ale *'as per the statute'*.

It seems that Catton's gaming transgression of 1633 had further repercussions for the alehouse keeper. A male called Henry Leigh from Halewood sought to indict him to appear at the Lancaster Assizes for the offence. Why Leigh did this is unknown, but whatever the reason, he had Catton brought before the higher court. Catton duly lodged an appeal against the indictment, and argued that the gaming, which was described as *'some carding for ale'* and which Catton stated had taken place *'unknowing to him'*, had been dealt with by the Little Woolton Manor Court with the fine already paid to the town's bailiff. In the appeal papers Catton claimed that Leigh's indictment was *'grounded in malice which the petitioner can here readily prove.'* Catton goes on to ask the presiding Justice of the Peace to *'stand with right and acquit'.* The evidence Catton gave and the result of the appeal are not recorded. However, the judgement may have been favourable, as his ability to carry on his trade remained unaffected.

(Fig.29) Overlay onto a satellite view of the Netherley area showing the course of the original roads and the proposed location of David Catton's alehouse. Image © Google Earth

In April 1634 Catton was brought before the manor court for selling ale by the quart which was only actually a pint and a half, and was fined 3 shillings and 4 pence (fellow alehouse keeper James Welling was similarly fined at the same time). In October the same year, the alehouse keeper was again before the court for his transgressions. Catton was fined 2 shillings for keeping ale that was *'neyther good nor holesome for man's bodie'.* The aletasters had clearly not found a lot to like about Catton's beer.

It seems Catton avoided sanction over the next few years, as he doesn't appear before the court again until 1638 when he was fined for not keeping his assize of bread and ale. This is Catton's last appearance in the records of the court, so it is unclear how long after this he kept his alehouse for.

The precise location of Catton's alehouse is never given, however records around the time refer to a house and three acres of land called Catton's Field or Catton's Hey. Subsequent transfer of ownership and occupancy indicates that it stood on the old Belle Vale Road, in modern day Netherley. There is no evidence that Catton's house remained an alehouse after his time there. In 1642 Catton's Hey was inherited by Richard Wainwright from his father Henry. The house and land came into the occupation of Robert Nodsby, and eventually the house became known or rebuilt as Garden Lodge.

In the 20th century the area was remodelled with new roads and housing estates. The old section of road upon which Catton's house stood was built over, and the new Childwall Valley Road was built a short distance to the south. The site of Catton's alehouse and the original section of road it stood upon is buried beneath modern development.

SKILLINGTON HOUSE

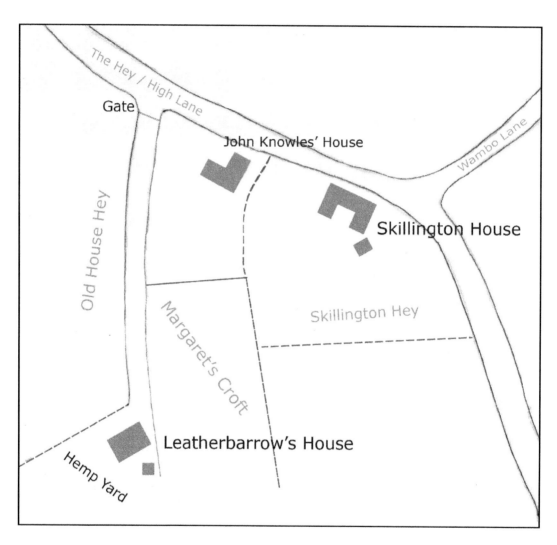

(Fig.30) Map showing the location of the alehouses of Edmund Webster (Skillington House) and Margerie Leatherbarrow in the mid-17th century. What was known as the Hey Lane or High Lane is Belle Vale Road, Old House Hey became the site of St Stephen's Church and Church Cottages were built on the site of John Knowles' House.

Skillington House was a Tudor period house which stood on modern day Belle Vale Road, opposite the junction with Wambo Lane and near to the site where Church Cottages now stand. It is long gone, having been demolished and built over with modern housing.

The Skillington family were amongst the earliest land owners of Little Woolton following the reformation and the seizure of the lands from the Knights Hospitallers. Peter Skillington was granted land by King Henry VIII in 1538, and these lands stood around the area of modern-day Belle Vale Road opposite to where Wambo Lane was later established. Even then the road was a main route to Warrington and Widnes.

A house was erected on the land, which in 1570 was shown as consisting of 2 acres, which was owned by James Skillington who rented it to his son Peter for 6s 8d per year. The house and attached land remained in the ownership of the Skillingtons into the 17th century. Unsurprisingly, it became known as Skillington House, a name it retained over the centuries that followed. The last Skillington to own the house was John Skillington, who died in 1621. Upon his death the house and land was purchased by John Cooke, who owned other land in the area, though John Skillington's widow Ellenor initially remained as tenant.

In 1624, the lane that came to be called Wambo Lane was established opposite Skillington House. In the court rolls that year it was noted that after the division of the common land, there was space left for a common lane of 8 yards in breadth from the lane by Skillington's House to Cockshed Brook and so to the house of Richard Cockett[1].

There is no evidence that the Skillington family had kept the house as a tavern or alehouse, as no member of the family appears as an innkeeper or victualler in the early records of the Little Woolton Manor. Succeeding Ellenor Skillington as the occupant of the house was William Deane, and upon his death, his son Nathaniel. The Deanes did not run the house as a tavern either, but that changed when licensed victualler Edward Webster and his wife Elizabeth became tenants of Skillington House in 1639. They acquired the house and three roods[2] of attached land, paying a yearly rent to John Cooke of 2 shillings and 6d.

The Websters appeared to run their alehouse without much trouble until in 1647 Edward was fined by the manor court for breaking his assize of bread and ale. In 1648, Webster found himself in dispute with his landlord John Cooke. It was customary each year for the Little Woolton manor court to elect a constable from amongst the chief land and property owners of the township. In 1648 it was deemed the turn of John Cooke to hold the office, however he refused to carry out the role, and instead delegated it to his tenant Edward Webster. Webster lodged an appeal with the assize court in Wigan, outlining the reasons why he should not be required to be Little Woolton's constable. Within his petition, Webster stated that Cooke owned and resided at a mansion house and several acres of estate within the township, while he rented just a meagre three roods of land from Cooke. Cooke was therefore far more obligated and qualified to be constable than he. Webster also argued that he had '*a great family to maintayne out of small means in these hard and heavy times*'. He could little afford the personal cost of being constable, as he had his livelihood to attend to. Webster appealed to the higher court to discharge him from the burden imposed upon him by Cooke, and for Cooke to be ordered to execute the constableship as he ought. It appears the court were only partly sympathetic to Webster's plea, as he and Cooke were ordered to share the role for the ensuing twelve months.

It seems sharing constableship did not unduly affect Webster or his ability to make a living. In 1649, 1651 and 1655 Webster appeared before the manor court for breaking the assize of bread and ale. In 1658 he was presented to the court for permitting unlawful gaming in his house. Those responsible were William Bushell of Much Woolton and William Pickering of Halewood, who were each fined 1 shilling and 4 pence for gaming with cards.

In 1659 Webster was in trouble with the court again, this time for suffering Thomas Eccleston, Edward Cockett and James Harrison to drink at his house on the Sabbath day. He was also presented for breaking the assize of bread and ale. Webster was guilty of this offence several more times in the 1660s, and in 1662 was fined for allowing William Ryecroft, William Houlgreave and his own son, William Webster, to play cards in his house.

Edward Webster died in 1680 and Skillington House came into the ownership of John Burgess from Toxteth. Burgess paid £270 to the then owner Thomas Cooke for the house and several pieces of the surrounding land. There is no evidence that the house was ever licensed again, and it stayed in the hands of the Burgess family until the mid-18th century.

Skillington House and the surrounding land eventually found its way into the ownership of Thomas Molyneux, and was demolished in the 19th century. A house called Lee Vale was built on the site. Echoes of the original old house and the family who built it could still be found in the mid-19th century in the name of a nearby field of five acres off Belle Vale Road which was called Skillington's Field. The old houses have since been demolished, and a housing estate occupies the land where Lee Vale, and before it Skillington House, had stood for centuries previously. No trace of the house of the Skillington family and alehouse of Edward Webster remain.

Notes:

[1] The earliest record of the lane being called Wambo Lane is in 1747, though the name likely predates this. The old Wambo Lane was eventually lost during the 20th century when development in the area brought a shopping centre, supermarket, car park and modern housing estate. The lane stretched all the way to Gorsey Cop farm, but only the first 10 yards of the original Wambo Lane still remains.

[2] A rood is a measurement of land equivalent to a quarter of an acre. Three roods would therefore be three quarters of an acre.

THE OLD HOUSE

(Fig.31) The lane that once led to Leatherbarrow's 17th century alehouse stands between St Stephen's Church and the Church Cottages built in 1872 by Andrew Barclay Walker. The lane, which leads to a modern housing estate, has now grassed over and serves to provide access to the cottages on the left.

In 1633, William and Marjory Gill held a messuage called the Old House, a hemp yard, and an area of attached land referred to as the Old House Hey. This year is the earliest indication that the house was an alehouse, as William Gill is fined for *'keeping ale(house) without licence'*.

In 1641, Henry Leatherbarrow acquired the house and land. Manorial court records, which contain orders for the maintenance of ditches and hedges between properties, indicate that the Old House was on land adjacent to Edward Webster's Skillington House. The house and yard was at the end of a small lane leading from the Hey Lane (modern day Belle Vale Road) and which corresponds with the footpath which currently separates St Stephen's Church from Church Cottages.

Shortly after acquiring the house, Leatherbarrow leased the Old House Hey and hemp yard to Edmund Wainwright who was the lease holder and licensee of the inn which was to become the Childwall Abbey. Given that Wainwright's inn in Childwall had its own brew house, and that there is no evidence of the Old House having one, it is possible that Wainwright supplied the Old House with its beer. The Leatherbarrows remained as occupants of the house, and when Henry Leatherbarrow died in around 1647, his son Edmund was recognised as his heir. The same year Henry's widow Marjorie was presented before the Manor Court for breaking the assize of bread and ale and fined.

Marjorie Leatherbarrow and her son Edmund remained as the occupants of the Old House, and in 1651 they were ordered to lay paving along the lane leading from the highway to their garden, and also to ensure that access to the lane from Belle Vale Road remained open.

It appears that Marjorie Leatherbarrow ran an orderly alehouse, as she is rarely presented before the manorial court for licensing offences. The Old House remained in the occupation of the Leatherbarrow family after the death of Marjory, though it seems the alehouse licence died with her. The house and land changed hands numerous times over the years that followed. The house was eventually demolished and in the 20th century the site of the Old House was built over with modern housing. The associated land known as Old House Hey is now the location of St Stephen's Church.

ROSAMUND FINCH'S TAVERN

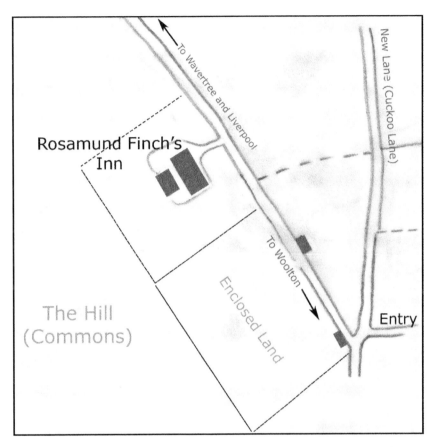

(Fig.32) Map showing the location of the tavern of Rosamund Finch around 1750. The inn was on modern day Woolton Road, but was replaced in the late 18th century by a house called Rose Hill, built by Thomas Rawson.

When Isaac Greene became Lord of the Manors of Little Woolton and Childwall in 1718, he set about enclosing and building upon parts of the commons. As well as a new manor house called Childwall Hall, Greene built himself a summer house near the highest point of Woolton Hill, and enclosed 3 acres of land on the hill near to the road from Woolton to Liverpool. Upon this land was erected a house which he leased to widow Rosamund Finch. This house became an inn or tavern, and Finch was its licensee.

Rosamund Finch, also referred to as 'Rose' and 'Rosa', was granted the lease in the 1740s. The lease was for the duration of her life, and that of her son James Finch who was a butcher. The premises consisted of a house and outbuildings with a garden and croft, and two fields of just over and acre each. Finch paid Greene £2 and 8 shillings per year rent.

Finch was recorded as holding a victuallers licence when records of the alehouse recognizances began in 1753, and was licensed each year until 1759. After this, being at this time in her 70s, she appears to retire from the licensing trade, as she is not shown as holding a licence thereafter. If her inn or tavern had a name, it has been lost to time and may never be known. Rosamund Finch died in 1768 and was buried in the graveyard of Childwall Church. James Finch continued to live at the house, though he never operated it as an inn. In 1775 he gave the lease up, and it was acquired by local landowner James Gildart.

By 1782 the leasehold of the house and land changed hands again being acquired by Benjamin Sandford, and in 1791 the property passed to Thomas Rawson. Rawson demolished Rosamund Finch's old tavern, and replaced it with a grand new house which he called Rose Hill, and which gave the nearby Rose Brow its name. The new house was named after Rose Hill in Liverpool which Rawson also owned. Rawson acquired other lands and property in Little Woolton, including the Holt estate. However, he chose to rent out the Holt to tenants, while he and his family lived at Rose Hill. In 1796 Rawson enclosed more of the common land on the hill, enlarging the Rose Hill estate further.

(Fig.33) Above: Contemporary drawing of Thomas Rawson's Rose Hill c1815 by J. Hindley. Used with permission of the Liverpool Record Office, Liverpool Libraries. Rose Hill was built on the site of Rosamund Finch's tavern. (Fig.34) Below: The same site today on Woolton Road is called Rosehill Court.

Upon his death in 1815, Rose Hill was inherited by Rawson's son, Thomas Rawson Junior. Following Rawson junior's death in 1847, the estates were acquired by Francis Henry Froes. Over the years that followed, further changes of ownership ensued until, in the mid-20th century, Rose Hill was demolished. Modern apartments, which go by the name of Rosehill Court, now stand upon the site. Any traces of Rosamund Finch's 18th century tavern have long since disappeared.

THE HALEWOODS OF THE GATE ACRE

(Fig.35) Paradise Row on Grange Lane, Gateacre. The part of the building with the porch (a more modern addition) was an alehouse from at least 1634 until 1647, and was occupied by Gwen Halewood, John Bennett and Henry Halewood in this period. The single fronted house just beyond it was the house of James Bane, who is recorded in the manor court rolls from 1617, and who served in several roles for the manor court of Little Woolton until his death in 1639, including Constable, Aletaster and, due to the convenient location of the house, Hill Looker. The building most likely predates 1617, and may even be late 16th century.

The name Halewood has a long connection with alehouses and inn keeping in Gateacre, with successive generations of the same family having kept inns in Little Woolton for over a century and a half. Over the course of the 17th century, the Halewoods occupied and operated several different licensed houses situated on the Gate Acre and Grange Lane.

The Gate Acre was an area of land on the corner of Grange Lane and Gateacre Brow which was part of the Grange estate. As early as 1553 there is an alehouse recorded as being here, when, in the manor court of William Norris, John Fletcher was fined for keeping unlawful gaming in his house, and for breaking the assize of bread and ale. The location of Fletcher's house can be determined due to the fact that in 1555, Fletcher and several other local residents are instructed to conduct repairs to the Churchway (an ancient name for Grange Lane) from the house of John Fletcher along to the Cockshead estate, an area of land bordering Childwall. This places the house in the same location as the house that was later occupied by the Halewoods, and it is entirely possible that it is one and the same, especially considering how few houses existed in the area at the time.

By 1584, Fletcher had died, and a member of the Halewood family appears in the manorial records for the first time in relation to licensing. William Halewood is fined for keeping unlawful gaming in his house, though it is not at this time specified where his house stood. After 1587 there is a gap in the records of the Little Woolton Manor Court, before they commence again in 1616. In 1618 both a William Halewood and a Henrie Halewood were fined by the court for keeping unlawful gaming in their houses, though once again locations are not given for their premises. In 1622, however, Thomas Halewood begins to appear in the court rolls and from this point there is some continuity in the history of his alehouse. There are numerous references to the Halewoods being '*of the Gate Acre*', and their house around this time was described as 'Halewood's Little House'. There are also indications that it stood near to the gate across Grange lane which possibly gave the Gate Acre its name.

Even in rural and sparsely populated Little Woolton life could be colourful and eventful, and nowhere did it appear to be more so than at Halewood's alehouse. Thomas Halewood found himself being presented before the manor court numerous times. On several occasions he was fined for the common transgression of not keeping the assize of bread and ale, and for keeping unlawful gaming in his house. He was also, it seems, negligent in renewing his alehouse licence on more than one occasion. In October 1622, Halewood was fined for keeping unlawful gaming in his house, and for keeping an alehouse without a licence '*since the last court until lent*'. In 1623 Halewood was fined for '*keeping an alehouse since the last court without licence*'. He was also fined 12d for harbouring his neighbours' servants (most likely the servants of Henry Orme of the Grange) in his house at an inconvenient time of the night, and also for not keeping the assize of white bread. In 1624 several people were caught gaming in Halewood's house, and all those involved, including the licensee himself, were fined. Halewood was also presented to the court for having a fight with William Bridge, with both men being fined 12d each.

In 1625, such was the seeming widespread reluctance of the township's alehouse keepers to renew their licences, the court felt compelled to specifically order that no one shall make or hold any ale for sale within the manor without a licence, upon pain of ten shillings. Despite this order, in 1626 Thomas Halewood was again before the court for selling ale without a licence as well as for suffering unlawful gaming and keeping a '*misguided woman*' in his house.

In April 1627, Thomas Halewood had a busy time in the manor court. He was presented to the court for not keeping the due assize of ale. He was also fined for harbouring and lodging '*wanderinge inconvenient persons*', and for harbouring a woman called Elizabeth Fletcher '*in the tyme of her chyld birth*'. At the same court, Halewood was again fined for '*harbouringe men's sons and servants at unreasonable tymes and unconvenient manner*'. Clearly the displeasure of the manorial court, of which Henry Orme was a prominent member, had been aroused by Halewood allowing certain individuals to carouse at his alehouse into the small hours. Halewood was fined the standard sum of 12 pence for each offence.

(Fig.36) Also part of Paradise Row, this addition to the original building, now two separate cottages, existed in some form at the time of James Bane and formed what was described as the 'lower end' of Bane's House. In 1639, widow Alice Whitfield and her daughter lived here for a short time.

By the 1630s, the Halewood family came to occupy another house nearby. This house was part of a row of dwellings which is currently known as 'Paradise Row'. The building was owned by Henry Orme of the Grange, and one of the houses was occupied by James Bane and was known as Bane's House. Another of the houses was occupied by Gwen Halewood, who, in 1634 was presented before the court for selling ale without a licence.

By 1635 alehouse keeper Thomas Halewood had died and there is no evidence that the Little House by the gate remained an alehouse. However, the house occupied by Gwen Halewood was a licensed house for the next decade or more. In 1637, Gwen was brought before the manor court for entertaining a strange woman in her house who was suspected as being a '*lewd woman*' and was also punished for not sending her away when warned by the constables. She was fined 3s and 4d.

In 1639, James Bane died, and the full row of houses was acquired by James Halewood as chief tenant, but he was soon to find himself in hot water with the manor court for taking under tenants without due authority. This included the house occupied by Gwen Halewood. That year the alehouse had a new occupant in James Bennett, but his tenancy had not been duly authorised. This did not prevent him from being presented for breaking the size of bread and ale, and permitting unlawful gaming in the house. Those that were found gaming were his landlord James Halewood, John Welling, James and William Allenson, William Pickering of Much Woolton and 'Little Henrie Halsall' of Childwall. Bennett was fined 12d for the assize offence and 3s 4d for permitting gaming. James Halewood was himself fined for permitting John Bennett to be his tenant being *'forbidden by the constables'*.

Six months later, in April 1640, Halewood appears in the court rolls *'for letting the house called Banes House to a stranger as a cottage, for letting Gwen Halewood's House unto John Bennett he being forbidden by the Constables, for letting Alice Whitfield widow in the lower end of Banes House'*. In addition to being fined, Halewood was ordered to eject Bennett from his premises. Alice Whitfield and her daughter, and John Fowler the stranger, were ordered *'to away the towne att or before the first day of May next.'*

Replacing Bennett in 1640 was Henry Halewood, son of deceased alehouse keeper Thomas Halewood. He immediately found himself presented and fined for failing to keep the assize of ale and permitting unlawful gaming in his house. He was fined a grand total of 7 shillings and 12 pence for the offences. The gamers on this occasion were James and William Allenson, James Halewood, William Crosse, and John Molineux. Henry Halewood was again fined in 1642 for failing to keep his assize of bread and ale.

By 1647 Henry Halewood had died, and Gwen Halewood had taken on the running the alehouse once more. She was fined by the court that year for brewing beer without a licence, and also for *'drawing and uttering brandy'* without a licence.

During the interregnum of 1649 to 1660, following the English Civil War, Halewood's house, along with all the other alehouses in Little Woolton except one, appears to have ceased operating. It was not until after the restoration of the monarchy that the Halewood name begin to appear again in the reports presented by the township's aletasters. In 1666 a Henry Halewood found himself before the court for breaking the assize of ale. By this time the Halewood family were occupying other, larger premises further along Grange Lane and opposite Henry Orme's Grange (see Fig. 8). The house was also owned by Orme with the Halewoods his tenants. The Grange had a brew house, and so was ideally placed to supply Halewood's tavern with ale. The little house by the gate, and the former Bane's House were occupied by other tenants. At some point Halewood's Little House became a smithy and the gate across the lane became known as 'Smithy Gate'.

Henry Halewood was fined for assize offences each year thereafter up until 1671, and several times in the early 1680s. By 1686, Halewood had left the old house on Grange Lane, and had taken occupancy of the Pinfold House (which much later became the Bridge Inn on Belle Vale Road) where he continued to ply his trade.

By 1687 the alehouse opposite the Grange, which was now owned by the Broughton family who also owned Childwall House, was described as *'the house late in the possession of Henry Halewood'*. In 1690, widow Mary Broughton was ordered to take up and drain away the water from the hill which flowed into the entryway to Halewood's old house. The 'entry way' still exists to this day as a public right of way allowing pedestrian access from Woolton Road to Grange Lane via Grange Weint. By 1695, Halewood's house had a new occupant in Thomas Barton who was presented for assize of ale offences. Given the convenient location of the house, Barton was also elected a hill looker for that year. Barton appears before the court only this once, so it is not clear how long he kept the house as an alehouse.

By 1705, Halewood's old house and the land it sat upon had a new owner in William Whitfield. There is no evidence that it was still an alehouse at this time, appearing to have fallen out of use as such. The house saw a number of tenants and occupiers over the decades that followed, but was never licensed again. Still standing in the late 1700s, by the early 1800s it had been demolished. The area where Halewood's old house once stood remained open land for the rest of the 19th century.

In the 20th century Grange Lane underwent new development, and modern housing was built on the site of Halewood's alehouse opposite the Grange. Halewood's Little House is also long gone, as is Smithy Gate. However, the houses once occupied by Gwen Halewood and James Bane are still standing. Now called Paradise Row, it is Gateacre's most complete survivor of early manorial Little Woolton.

(Fig.37) Public footpath at the junction of Cuckoo lane and Woolton Road leading to Grange Weint. Once the 'entry way' leading to Halewood's Old House opposite the original Grange on Grange Lane, there has been a right of way here since at least the 1600s.

THE TALBOT / THE DOG

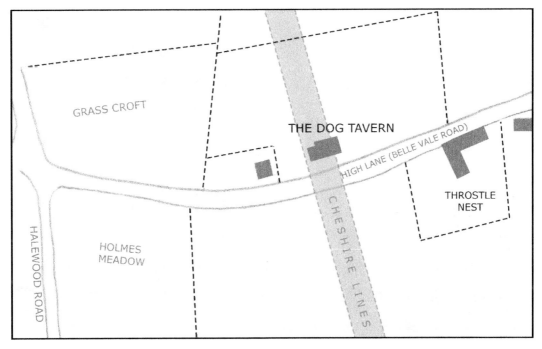

(Fig.38) Map of Belle vale Road in the 18th century showing the location of the inn known as the Talbot and later the Dog. The shaded section indicates where the Cheshire Lines Railway was later built, and where the Liverpool Loopline cycle path is located today.

The inn recorded as both the 'Talbot' and the 'Dog' stood on what is now Belle vale Road for over 40 years in the mid to late 18th century. The old building which became the inn had its origins back in the 17th century.

The manor of Little Woolton was, in the 16th century, owned by the Earl of Derby, and was under the local stewardship of the Norris family of Speke. The Norris family held by copyhold 6 and a half acres of land near to the Gate Acre, on what was the main highway through the township.

The first mention of the property is in the manorial rolls of 1633, when William Norris is recorded as having died and left six and a half acres of land in Little Woolton to his son and heir, William Norris the younger. In 1634, the land and a house which stood upon it, was in the occupation of Richard and Jane Lawrenson. When William Norris junior died, the land and house were inherited by his son Thomas Norris, and in 1667 Ellinor Gill, the daughter of Richard and Jane Lawrenson, paid Norris £26 to take occupancy. However, by 1670 the house and land were in the occupancy of Richard Wainwright, and it stayed with the Wainwright family into the 18th century.

Ownership of the property was passed down the Norris line, until, in the mid-18th century, it was under the ownership of Mary Beauclerk. In 1751, Henry Halewood took occupancy of the house and tenement that had become known as 'Wainwrights near Gateacre', paying 6 shillings and sixpence rent to Beauclerk. Halewood was a licensed victualler, and the house became an inn or tavern. Halewood's house was named in the alehouse recognizances of 1773 as the Talbot. In 1775, the house and land was purchased from the Beauclerk estate by Henry Grace. By 1777, the name of the house had been changed to the Dog, possibly by the new owner. Licensee Henry Halewood died in 1778, and his wife Margaret took over the licence. Margaret ran the Dog for three years, but by 1781 the house was licensed to Henry Kelshaw. Kelshaw was a butcher, and as well as running the alehouse had a slaughter house and shop on Halewood Road.

Grace was not the owner of the tenement for long, and by 1783 it had changed hands, being acquired by James Roberts, and then in 1784 by Thomas Smyth. Smyth also owned Belle Vale House, and the Dog sat upon his estate. With the new owner came a new tenant and licensee in Henry Sherwood. Sherwood ran the Dog until 1787, when the licence was not renewed. By 1788, the estate had been acquired by Thomas Whitwell.

Although the house remained standing, it was not licensed again, and instead was occupied by a series of tenant farmers. Being part of the Belle Vale estate, it is shown in maps dating from the 1840s as Belle Vale Farm. The old house formerly known as the Talbot and the Dog, and the land it stood upon, was eventually acquired by the Cheshire Lines Committee in the 1870s, and the former inn was demolished to make way for the Cheshire Lines railway line. The railway itself is now defunct, but the location of the old inn is marked by the railway bridge over Belle Vale Road, with the actual site buried beneath the embankment of earth which once held the railway tracks and station, but which is now the Liverpool Loopline footpath and cycle path.

THE BLACK BULL

(Fig.39) The Black Bull Inn photographed around 1900. In the doorway can be seen the figure of licensee Alice Martin. This view of the inn and Gateacre Brow has hardly changed since this time.

The Black Bull, also at one time known as the Bull Inn, stands on Gateacre Brow near to the junction with Grange Lane, and is one of the oldest surviving inns in the area. The appearance of the building we see today, with its mock Tudor façade, can be attributed to Andrew Barclay Walker who made the alterations in 1887. However, the inn predates Walker's ownership by almost a century and a half, and was formed from a couple of buildings that can be traced back even further, to at least the middle of the 17th century.

The land on what is now Gateacre Brow, near to the junction with Grange Lane, once belonged to the Grange estate, and was known as the Gate Acre. Part of the land was open, common or waste land. This common land was at the corner where the two roads met, and there was a pool or pond upon it known locally as the Creep Hole[1]. The Gate Acre was owned freehold, which meant it could be bought and sold by its owners without having to defer to the lord of the manor or the manorial court. The early history of the Gate Acre can therefore be more difficult to ascertain than that of copyhold property, however the court rolls do hold some clues. Exactly when the house that was to become part of the Black Bull was built is unclear, but it can be traced to at least the time the Walton family were owners of the land.

The name Walton has been associated with Little Woolton since the earliest post reformation times. In the court rolls commencing in 1547, Peter Walton is shown as a prominent member of the township's inhabitants and in the late 16th century holds various roles as an officer of the court. It is clear that even at this time Walton holds land, and possibly a house, on or near the Gate Acre, as in 1555 he is compelled by the manorial court to contribute to the maintenance of Grange Lane. By 1617 it is Richard Walton who is shown as a landowner or chief tenant within the town, also holding several positions, most notably as supervisor of the highways. However, in 1640 Walton is elected as a hill looker for the first time. It made practical sense that the role of hill looker be given to someone living near Woolton Hill and this seems generally to have been the case. Again, this suggests that the Walton family already inhabited the land at the Gate Acre which they were later shown to own, and that the house that was later to form part of the Black Bull, or an early version of it, was already in existence. Richard Walton died in 1663, and his son Peter Walton was his heir. At this time the Waltons also had a house and three acres of copyhold land on the outskirts of the Lee estate. By 1680, Peter Walton had also died, and his freehold and copyhold estates were inherited by his son Richard.

There is clear indication around this time as to where the freehold house and land belonging to Richard Walton stood. In 1690 Walton was ordered to cut his thorn hedge between his land and that of Alice Davis who owned Abbot's House, which stood on the north-west corner of Gateacre Brow and was to become the site of the New or Higher Grange. In 1696, Richard Walton was ordered by the court to '*make a sufficient fence betwixt the close commonly called Walton's Close and the lane going to Childwall*'. This locates the house and land on the Gate Acre, where the Black Bull stands today. The house, due to its location, became known as the Gate Acre House. Although other houses would claim the name 'Gateacre House' in later centuries, Walton's house was the first to hold this title. The house remained in the occupation of the Walton family up until the early 18th century. In 1707, Richard Walton died, and he asked in his will for his freehold house and four acres of attached land to be sold to pay his debts. His copyhold near the Lee was left in the hands of his widow Ellen, while the Gate Acre House and land was bought by the Orme family of the original or Lower Grange.

As well as Walton's house, another building plays a part in the history of what would eventually become the Black Bull. In 1658, Peter Legay bought Childwall and Little Woolton Manors, and although Little Woolton's manor court had been active from the 16th century, the manor court of Childwall had been dormant for many decades. Legay revived the Childwall court, and as Childwall had a much lower population than Little Woolton, Legay combined the two courts, holding a single court for the two townships twice a year. The court of Little Woolton had been held at the Holt for many years, but with the court now combined with Childwall, a more centrally located court was needed. A new court house was built on the common land at the corner of Gateacre Brow and Grange Lane, opposite the Creep Hole. The small court house was in use for the rest of the 17th century, standing near to, and parallel with, the Gate Acre House. The position of the two buildings, set at an angle to the road, appeared to have been dictated by the small body of water on the corner opposite them.

In 1703, Isaac Greene became steward of the manorial court, and, living in Childwall, he moved the Childwall court closer to home. The joint court of Childwall and Little Woolton was split, with the Little Woolton court returning to the Holt and the Childwall court initially being held at the house of Eleanor Abbot, the inn that was to become known as the Childwall Abbey. The court house by the Gate Acre crossroads fell out of use and was also acquired by the Orme family. Both the Gate Acre House and the former court house were later bought by

David Edwardson, who turned them into the Black Bull Inn.

Edwardson was originally a watch tool maker who lived in Much Woolton. He had married his wife Catherine in 1735, and they had a number of children, including a daughter called Margaret in 1743. By 1746 they had moved to Little Woolton, purchasing the Gate Acre House and the old former court house from the Orme family. Edwardson also rented a piece of land called Lawrenson's field, which was on Halewood Road near to the Nook estate. Edwardson used the collection of buildings he had acquired as one premises, with the house and former court house essentially becoming two 'wings', with another low building at their rear giving the premises the distinctive 'U' shape which appears on the earliest maps of the area. The former court was used as a parlour for customers, and Edwardson found himself in the unusual position of having to pay rent to the Lord of the Manor for this part of his house. The former court house, or parlour end of his house, having been originally built upon the commons, was administered differently than the freehold part of the house. Edwardson also paid rent for a small piece of land across the road, next to Gateacre Chapel.

In 1753, the recording of the issuing of alehouse licences was made compulsory by law, and David Edwardson appears in the recognizance rolls as the licensee of the inn. The name of the inn was not included in the records at this time, but when its name was first recorded in 1773 it is shown as the Black Bull. Despite this, Edwardson's inn was still recorded for administrative purposes in the manorial records as the Gate Acre House and the Court House up to the end of the century.

(Fig.40) A sketch of the Bull Inn in around 1815 by J.Hindley. The former court house can be seen far right, while Gateacre chapel is far left. The 'Creep Hole' pond is in the foreground, while the Bear and Ragged Staff is partially obscured by the Bull's roadside sign. The land where the pond is situated was, in 1887, gifted to the people of Gateacre by the Victorian owner of the Black Bull, Andrew Barclay Walker, and is now Gateacre Green. Used with permission of the Liverpool Record Office, Liverpool Libraries.

In March 1779 Edwardson's wife Catherine died, with Edwardson himself dying in March 1782. The Edwardsons' daughter Margaret took over the running of the inn. Following David Edwardson's death, the actual ownership of the Black Bull rested in the hands of his executors, until it was eventually acquired by Thomas Riding in 1785. Despite the change of ownership, Margaret Edwardson remained as tenant and licensee until 1795, when her brother in law, Thomas Shephard, took over. Shephard, a watchmaker, had married Catherine, Margaret Edwardson's sister, in 1758. Shephard only held the license for two years. In 1797 he died, leaving his wife Catherine to take on the licence.

Following the local Enclosures Act of 1805[2], the common land with its pond, opposite the Black Bull, was allotted to the inn's owner, becoming part of the property of the inn, though the area would later be gifted back to the township as Gateacre Green. Licensee Catherine Shephard died in 1805, and Jonathan Tatlock became the new tenant of the inn. Tatlock, who was also a saddler by trade, was to run the inn for three decades. It was during Tatlock's tenure that the Black Bull became known as the Bull Inn, appearing as such in Baines' Lancashire Directory in 1825 and other local property notices around the same time.

By 1838, Tatlock, who appears to have been a confirmed bachelor and had no children, had retired from the trade. He remained in Gateacre, and died in 1844. His successor as licensee of the Bull Inn was Charles Davies, who had been the licensee of the Horse and Jockey public house in Roby. But by 1840, Davies found himself bankrupt, and appeared before the insolvency court in Lancaster in July that year. By 1841, Davies had left his positon at the Bull Inn, and was replaced by John Ramsay and his wife Ellen. Ramsay had formerly managed a tavern in Ditton, but his tenure at the Bull Inn was short-lived indeed. On 11th January 1842, after only a few months in charge, John Ramsay died and his wife Ellen was granted transfer of the licence.

On 22nd July 1845 Ellen Ramsay married Thomas May, and May promptly took over as licensee. Thomas May, originally from Carlisle in Cumberland, was a cabinet maker by trade. Although his name was on the licence, it was his wife Ellen who ran the inn, while May focused on his joinery business.

Around the time that May took the licence for the Bull Inn, the premises came under the ownership of Henry Fleetwood. Fleetwood, still only a young man in his twenties, was the son of the late John Fleetwood who had built the nearby Gateacre Brewery. It was during the era of the Fleetwoods that substantial alterations were made to the inn. The former court house part of the premises was knocked down, and an extension built to the side of the main house. The distinctive 'U' shape had now gone, with the inn becoming the double fronted building it still is today.

On 22nd November 1846, Thomas May found himself summonsed by Inspector Webb of the local police charged with permitting drunkenness and disorder at the Bull. Appearing at Prescot Court in December, May pleaded his innocence, stating that the person who was causing the disturbance in the inn was none other than its owner Henry Fleetwood. This, claimed May's lawyer, placed the licensee in an awkward position, as he couldn't very well order the owner to leave his own inn. The chair of the bench was inclined to dismiss the case on this information, however his fellow magistrates disagreed, and stated that the presence of the landlord was no justification. May was fined 20 shillings and 6d, while Fleetwood and six other persons who had been present at the time were all fined for drunkenness.

On 12th July 1851, May was summonsed again for permitting disorder and drunkenness at the Bull, though this time the owner was not involved. Appearing at Prescot Court on 5th August, May was fined 5 shillings plus costs. It is not known whether May's conviction was directly connected, but on the same day, transfer of the licence for the Bull Inn was granted to James Ratcliffe.

In August 1851, owner Henry Fleetwood died and in January 1852 the Bull Inn was offered for sale by auction. At the time, the property included the former common land in front of the inn, as well as stables and 1331 square yards of land at the rear. Following the auction, the property remained in the ownership of the Fleetwood family. The Black Bull, along with the brewery and the Brown Cow beer house, was acquired by George Fleetwood the younger, whose father owned the Tarbock Brewery.

In 1869, the Bull Inn played its part in what was a rather macabre incident. On 25th August that year, game keeper John Lloyd, who was in the employ of the owner of Childwall Hall, was passing through a section of land known as the Black Nursery when he came across the corpse of a man. The flesh on the body had been eaten away, revealing the skeleton, and it was clear the body must have lain there for several months. The clothing on the body consisted of Barragan trousers and waistcoat, white shirt, blucher boots, 'billycock' or bowler hat, dark coat and magenta scarf. The remains were placed in a coffin and were taken to the Bull Inn where they stayed while an inquest was arranged. The inquest was duly held at the inn, though the cause of death and identity of the deceased could not be ascertained. It was later believed that the body was that of a man called Jones, from Woolton, who had left the Prescot Workhouse some months earlier and had disappeared. How he came by has sad demise will likely never be known.

James Ratcliffe was to run the Bull for over 25 years. In December 1875, the inn was purchased by brewing magnate Andrew Barclay Walker, who lived at the nearby Higher Grange and who had also acquired the Gateacre Brewery and the Brown Cow beer house at the same time. Notices from the time of the auction show the inn as being called the 'Black Bull', though many other sources from the period and just afterwards show it to still be called the 'Bull'. In December 1876 James Ratcliffe moved on, and the licence for the Bull Inn was transferred to Alexander Martin, who took up residence with his wife Alice and their children. Martin was a member of the Devonshire Lodge of Freemasons. The Martin family's tenure at the inn was not to be without incident, and some tragedy, with their 4 year old daughter Alice dying on May 13th 1878.

In July 1881 a servant at the Bull Inn, a 14 year old girl called Catherine Moss, found herself in court charged with Arson at the premises. Part of Catherine's duties was to make the bed in the barman's room at the inn. Having done so on the afternoon of the 9th March that year, and having just left the room, smoke had been seen issuing from it. When this was investigated, it was found that the valance of the bed was on fire. This was extinguished, but smoke was then found to be coming from a nearby chest of drawers. Half burned matches and some other partially burned items were found in the drawer. Police Sergeant Peters was called to the scene to look into the matter. He established that the barman did not keep matches in his room, and upon questioning Catherine he elicited a statement from her admitting she had started the fire, though she stated she did so accidentally. She was charged with the offence of arson and appeared at the Liverpool Assizes in July. During the trial the facts were examined, but in his summing up the Judge made it clear that he did not like the way the vulnerable and rather naïve young girl had been dealt with or questioned by the Police Sergeant. The Sergeant stated that at the time it was not his intention to charge the girl with the offence, but was merely establishing the facts of the incident. On direction from the Judge the jury found Catherine not guilty and she was acquitted. However, the ordeal was not quite over for her. She appeared back in Court a week later having been charged with setting fire to a stable at the inn in January 1881. The full circumstances behind this allegation are not known, but when she appeared back in court, the prosecution offered no evidence against her, and again she was acquitted.

In 1887 the owner of the Bull Inn, Andrew Barclay Walker, submitted plans to make alterations to the premises. It had become practice for the Walker family to rebuild, remodel and improve the buildings in the area in the late 19th and early 20th century. The mock Tudor façade and red brick extensions that were added to the Bull are similar to similar improvements that were made to the row of cottages next to the Bull Inn, the Brown Cow, and similar to the style in which the cottages next to St. Stephen's Church were built in 1872. Andrew Barclay Walker, and his son, William Hall Walker, did much to develop and improve their local village of Gateacre, and made a significant impact on how the village looks today.

On 28th September 1893, long standing licensee of the Bull Inn, Alexander Martin, died aged 59 years. His funeral took place at Anfield Cemetery in Liverpool, and was attended by a notable number of Gateacre residents. In December the licence was granted to his widow Alice. The same year, Andrew Barclay Walker also died, and Gateacre Grange and the other nearby properties he owned, which included the Bull Inn, were inherited by his son William Hall Walker. It was around this time that the inn's name reverted to the Black Bull, the name by which it has been known ever since.

On 26th August 1895, a male called Walter Williams attended the Black Bull Inn, drunk and demanding to be served. The barman refused to serve him due to his drunken state and Williams duly offered to fight the barman. A short time later PC Hamilton Taylor attended the inn, and taking hold of Williams forcibly 'put him outside', while reporting him for summons for being drunk on licensed premises. On 6th September Williams appeared in court on Quarry Street and was fined 20 shillings and costs for his trouble.

On Monday 16th November 1903, at half past six in the evening, two men called Thomas Cullen and Patrick Horan, both labourers who lodged together in Woolton, called at the Black Bull. Cullen was a habitual drunkard, and after being convicted of a drunkenness offence in May that year had been placed on the 'blacklist'. The Habitual Drunkards Act of 1898 had given the power to the courts to ban those convicted of multiple drunkenness offences from obtaining, or attempting to obtain any alcohol for a period of three years. Their names and photographs were placed on a list which was distributed by the police to all the licensed houses in the area. Upon entering the Black Bull, Horan went forward into the tap room of the house, while Cullen waited in the passage by the entrance. Horan ordered two pints of beer, and was served by William Martin, the licensee's son. The beer was placed on the counter, and Horan paid for it. Cullen then stepped forward, and was recognised immediately by Martin as being on the blacklist. He took the beer away from Cullen, and gave Horan the money back. When he told Cullen it was because he was barred from obtaining drink, Cullen denied it, stating that it was his brother who was on the list. He continued to deny it even when Martin brought out the photograph provided by the police and showed it to him. The men left the inn and went to Woolton, where they both got drunk and were later arrested. The case was heard at the court on Quarry Street on 4th December. Prosecuting, Superintendent Baxendale told the magistrates that Horan had been before the court 20 times previously for drunkenness offences, and Cullen 29 times, 3 of those since being placed on the blacklist. Cullen was fined 20 shillings for obtaining drink whilst banned, and Horan was fined 20 shillings for aiding and abetting him. Both men were also bound over to behave themselves for six months with a surety of £5 each.

Alice Martin ran the Black Bull for over a decade, until her own death on 10th August 1905 after a three week illness. In December 1905, George Wiggins took over the running of the inn. He was to remain as licensee until December 1909, when he was replaced by Henry Wild. Former book keeper Wild was 39 years old and unmarried, and ran the Black Bull with his brother, Robert. On 29th March 1912, Robert Wild became the licensee, but by 1914 the Black Bull had a new licensee in James Wicks, a former carpenter from Reading in Berkshire. Wicks went on to run the house for almost three decades.

In February 1916, a curious case occurred when Wicks and his wife Charlotte were sued for slander by a local cattle food salesman called William Stark from Halewood Road. The case stemmed from an incident in June 1915, when licensee Wicks accused Stark of stealing a handbag belonging to his sister in law, who worked behind the bar at the Black Bull. On 29th June, Stark had called at the inn and was served a drink by Kate Bennett, who was Charlotte Wicks' sister. Later, after Stark had left the Black Bull and made his way home, Bennett found her handbag to be missing. The bag had contained about £17 in cash. Stark claimed that James Wicks called to his house that evening and asked him what he had done with Miss Bennett's bag. Stark claimed no knowledge of the bag, and asked why he was thought to have taken it, to which Wicks replied, "Because you were the last man in the place." Wicks left, but a short time later his wife Charlotte and her sister called to the house, again accusing Stark of taking the bag, stating, "If you don't give it back, we shall put the matter in the hands of the police." Stark again denied the theft. With the accusations rankling in his mind, Stark returned to the Black Bull to confront Mrs Wicks. He told her that the charge she brought against him was a very serious matter, and she replied, "Yes, things look very black against you. You'll remember the affair of the gloves." Mrs Wicks was apparently referring to an incident on an earlier occasion at the Black Bull when a pair of gloves had been taken by some customers, passed around and then, as a joke, placed in Stark's pocket. Though it was accepted that Stark knew nothing of this, it had come to Stark's attention that Wicks was recently overheard saying that if Stark would steal a pair of gloves, then he would also steal a bag.

Stark was never prosecuted by the Police, but he argued that the accusation had tarnished his reputation and that he had lost friends and business because of it. He claimed did not want money out of the case, just an apology from Mr and Mrs Wicks. In their defence, the Wicks' lawyer claimed that the whole affair had been blown out of proportion by Stark. James Wicks had gone to visit him after the bag had disappeared because he thought Stark might have been playing another practical joke, not because he thought him a thief. Wicks further claimed that Stark had gone back to the Black Bull after the incident and had been annoying customers. He had been badgering them, wanting to know if anyone accused him of anything, to which they all replied they did not. Stark eventually had to be ejected from the inn. In cross examination, licensee Wicks denied making any accusation against Stark, or calling him a liar, and stated he had nothing to apologise for. The bag, incidentally, had never been found. The jury at the hearing found in Stark's favour, and awarded him £10 damages. The unsavoury litigation with William Stark did little to affect Wicks' own standing or reputation, and he was to continue as licensee of the Black Bull for many more years.

In 1917 William Hall Walker sold the whole of his estate and property holdings in Gateacre to Edgar Creyke Fairweather of Kingswear, Devon, who duly sold the Black Bull back to the Walker family's brewery, Peter Walker & Son of Warrington and Burton. In 1921 Walker's Brewery merged with Robert Cain & Sons to form Walker Cain.

By 1939 James Wicks, who was at this time 74 years old, had retired and was succeeded as licensee of the Black Bull by Thomas Formby, who held the licence through the war years. Throughout the 20th century, the companies that owned the inn merged and changed several times. Owners of the Black Bull in subsequent years included Tetley Walker, Allied Domecq, Punch Taverns, Bass Leisure, Six Continents and Mitchells and Butlers.

The Black Bull inn is still open for business and holds a commanding position in the centre of Gateacre Village. Although the interior has been refurbished a number of times, it has maintained more or less the same outward appearance for almost 150 years.

(Fig.41) The Black Bull Inn in Gateacre c1815, based on a contemporary sketch by J. Hindley © Stuart Rimmer

Notes:

[1]The pond of water known as the Creep Hole was later filled in, and is now the location of Gateacre Green. The Golden Jubilee Bust of Queen Victoria marks the spot where the pond stood. Gateacre Brow is referred to as the Creep Hole Lane at least once in the 17th century manorial records.

[2]Abridged for brevity. The full title of the 1805 Act was 'An Act for Inclosing Lands in the Manors or Townships of Childwall, Great Woolton and Little Woolton, in the Parish of Childwall, in the County Palatine of Lancaster.'

THE BEAR AND STAFF

(Fig.42) Gateacre Brow and the Bear and Ragged Staff c1815 based on a contemporary sketch by J. Hindley. The building has a design typical of the Georgian era, as opposed to the much earlier style of the nearby Black Bull. The inn was to be considerably enlarged and extended later in the 19th and early 20th centuries. To the top right is the 'New Grange' of Henry Fairclough, its grounds not yet enclosed by the high stone walls that were built later and added to by Andrew Barclay Walker. © Stuart Rimmer

The Bear and Staff stands on Gateacre Brow and has also been known as the Bear and Ragged Staff and the Bear Inn in the past. It is still in business today, and is one of the oldest surviving inns in the area. Although it is situated in the village of Gateacre, it was historically in the township of Much Woolton, on the border with Little Woolton.

The precise date the inn was built is unknown, but it is unlikely that it predates the Gateacre Chapel which was built in 1700 and was one of the first stone buildings on that side of the road. The inn has features consistent with the Georgian era, unlike the nearby Black Bull, which has architectural characteristics of an earlier period.

The earliest recorded owner and licensee of the inn was William Davies, who can be placed there from at least 1747, and who appears in the alehouse recognizances from 1753. The first time the name of the inn is recorded is in 1773, when it is shown as the 'Bear and Ragged Staff'.

The origin of the inn's name is not clear. The Bear and Ragged Staff was the heraldic emblem of the Earls of Warwick and featured on their coat of arms. Having been used by the Beauchamp family in ancient times, the emblem was granted to Francis Greville of Warwick Castle in 1760 after not being used for over a century. Greville died in 1773, by which time the inn in Gateacre already had its name. A story that the Earl had once stayed at the inn whilst on his travels, and was so impressed with the hospitality he received that he gave permission for his badge to be used as the inn's motif, is difficult to verify and may be apocryphal. However, if the inn is named after the Earl of Warwick, then prior to 1760 the house of William Davies would have had a different name which is lost to time.

William Davies was owner and licensee of the Bear and Ragged Staff until his death in 1775, when both the inn and the licence were inherited by his widow Ann. Ann Davies ran the inn herself until 1783, at which time she took a tenant by the name of Joshua Tyrer who took over the running of the establishment.

In 1789, Ann Davies died, and the Bear and Ragged Staff was purchased by the Reverend Thomas Forster, who owned other land and property in the area. With the new owner came a new tenant and licensee in the person of Joseph Webster. Webster did not run the inn for long, however, as he died in April 1793, leaving his widow Margaret to take over. Joseph Webster was buried in the graveyard of the nearby Gateacre Chapel.

In 1797 Margaret Webster had raised enough money to buy the Bear and Ragged Staff from Forster. She ran the inn for several decades until, in 1825, her son Richard took over the licence from his elderly and ailing mother. Margaret died on 4th December 1826 at the grand old age of 87 years, and her son became owner of the inn. Richard Webster was licensee of the Bear and ragged Staff until his death on 25th January 1834. After his death the inn was purchased by William Fleetwood, son of the late Eccleston brewer John Fleetwood. William Fleetwood had married Hannah Webster, the daughter of Richard, so the inn was essentially staying within the Webster family. However, it was the Fleetwood name that would become synonymous with the licence and brewing trade in Gateacre for the next half century. As well as buying the inn, William Fleetwood acquired the licence to run it himself. It was during this period that the name of the inn was changed from the Bear and Ragged Staff to simply the Bear Inn.

Fleetwood ran the inn for three years, until he died on 26th September 1837 aged only 36, and his widow Hannah Fleetwood took over the running of the house. She died in 1855 and ownership of the Bear Inn was acquired by her brother-in-law, brewer George Fleetwood from the Tarbock Brewery. The new licensee of the Bear Inn was John Gregory. Gregory was another name that would become connected with the brewing trade in Gateacre, though not for a few more years yet. He had been a clerk at the Tarbock brewery, working for George Fleetwood, and when his employer purchased the Bear Inn he was given the opportunity to acquire the licence.

John Gregory was licensee of the Bear Inn until 1864. At this point he moved on to run a beer house which he had purchased in Woolton, and the licence was transferred to a new tenant, widow Hannah Fairclough. Fairclough, originally from Widnes, was licensee of the Bear Inn until her death on 27th November 1868. She was succeeded by Edward Lawrenson, a former greengrocer from Upper Hill Street, Toxteth. However, his tenure was to be short. On 10th January 1871, Lawrenson died at only 32 years old. Transfer of the license was granted to his widow Anne.

Anne Lawrenson ran the Bear Inn until June 1873. She was replaced by Joshua Ledger, who was originally from Guildford in Surrey, and his wife Annie from Halewood. Tragedy struck the Ledgers while they were at the Bear Inn, when their son George died in September 1880 aged only 2 years. Ledger ran the Bear Inn until 1st February 1889, when Yorkshireman Aaron Robinson was granted transfer of the licence.

In July 1890, Robinson was hosting the local lodge of the Oddfellows, a members' cooperative and friendly society, which was holding its annual celebration at the inn. During the proceedings a theft occurred, when a man named Samuel Jones, a coachman of Cuckoo Lane, Gateacre, who was working as a waiter at the event, had his coat, valued at 30 shillings, and a key stolen. A young labourer, Isaac Killian of Rodick Street, Woolton, had gone into the bagatelle room of the inn and had taken the coat from the hook where it had been left. Jones later found his coat missing and notified the police. Killian had made his way to Garston where he pawned the coat for 4 shillings 6d at James Baron Pawnbrokers, 76 St Mary's Road. Acting on 'intelligence' the police attended Baron's shop where the coat was found with the missing key in the pocket. The police later arrested Killian, who was in still possession of the pawn ticket. On 18th July Killian appeared at Woolton Court where he pleaded guilty. He was sentenced to 14 days in prison.

On Sunday 22nd March 1891, licensee Robinson was assaulted at the Inn by a male by the name of Thomas Rigby. Rigby and several other men had entered the Bear but due to it being outside of permitted hours the licensee had refused to serve them. The men refused to leave, so Robinson had to forcibly eject them, during which Rigby struck him. Rigby appeared at Woolton Court on 3rd April and pleaded guilty to assault, expressing his regret at hitting Robinson. He was fined 10 shillings and costs.

On 7th December 1894, transfer of the licence for the Bear Inn was granted from Aaron Robinson to William Fleetwood. Once again, the old inn was in the hands of a member of the Fleetwood family. William was the son of former owners William and Hannah Fleetwood, and had been born and raised in the Bear Inn over half a century earlier. After the death of his mother, Fleetwood had remained in the brewery business and had been a buyer for Allsopp's Ales. Now, at the age of 60, he was returning to run the inn where he had been born. Amongst other things, Fleetwood set about revamping the bowling green of the Bear Inn, and having done so established a new bowling club there, which by August 1895 had over 40 members.

On 25th August 1899, at the licensing sessions at Woolton Court, the Police raised objections to the renewal of the license for the Bear Inn. The yard and stables of the inn were sub-let to John McLaughlin, who was licensee of the Brown Cow beer house. McLaughlin used the yard of the Bear Inn for his horse coach business. This made it difficult for the Police to effectively supervise the inn, and to distinguish between people who were entering the premises to make use of the coach business, or to access the inn outside of permitted hours. In order to examine the case in more detail, the bench adjourned Fleetwood's licence renewal hearing until September.

At the adjourned licensing sessions on 29th September a solution was suggested that met the approval of the court. Fleetwood would build a wall to separate the stables from the inn, and McLaughlin was to build some stables at the rear of the Brown Cow which would allow him to transfer his coach business to his own premises. On this basis, the licence for the Bear was renewed.

In March 1903, at the annual licensing sessions in Woolton, the local justices had decided to personally inspect all the licensed houses in the district. As with most of the houses, they had found the Bear Inn in need of some improvement. The toilet provision was inadequate and unsanitary, and access to it was through the kitchen of the premises. Although the rear yard was no longer shared with the coach business, it was too open and accessible to the public. The court required that the owners submit plans to rectify this situation.

On 7th August 1903, plans were submitted to the court offering solutions to the magistrates' concerns. A proper lavatory and urinal was to be constructed both on the ground floor and upstairs which did not require access through the private areas of the premises. The kitchen was to be closed off from the public area, and a new fully enclosed private yard was to be constructed which could only be accessed via the kitchen. The court approved the plans. By February 1904, work on the inn was still ongoing, with what were described as 'extensive alterations' being made to the house which, it was reported, would 'improve it greatly'.

On 3rd June 1904, at a special licensing session in Woolton, Edward Rylance applied for transfer of the licence for the Bear Inn. Alterations to the house had just been completed and William Fleetwood, now in his 70th year, had decided to move on. Fleetwood moved to live in Wavertree, but only 8 months later he died and was buried at St Peter's Church in Woolton.

Rylance had been resident of Gateacre for the past five years, and now looked to take up residency of the Bear. There was no objection from the police, and Rylance became the licensee. Rylance was not at the inn for long, however, and on 1st December 1905 the licence was granted to Alice Jones. It was also around this period that the name of the inn changed from the Bear to the Bear and Staff, the name it retains today.

Alice Jones was Licensee of the Bear and Staff for just under three years, and in September 1908 Edwin Morris became the new licensee of the inn. He was replaced on 30th September 1910 by William McCririe on a temporary basis, with his position as licensee being made permanent in February 1911.

On 3rd April 1913, Emily McCririe, the wife of the licensee, attended Woolton Court to apply for transfer of the licence from her husband. The court saw this as an 'unusual' application as it was not practice at the time for a woman to apply to take over a licence when her husband was still at the house. Lawyer W. Knowles stated that Mr McCririe was employed in Widnes, and that his wife had conducted the business at the Bear and Staff in his absence for some time, and had done so with no cause for complaint. William McCririe's work kept him away from the inn in the day, but he returned in the evenings. As there was no reason in law to deny the transfer, and there was no objection from the police, the application was granted.

On 2nd February 1914, at the first licensing session since Gateacre had been incorporated into the city of Liverpool, Emily McCririe attended Dale Street Magistrates Court to apply for renewal of her licence. She was made to give an undertaking similar to that asked of the other 'country' pubs in the area, which was that no drinks would be served on the bowling green or anywhere other than in the bar of the inn. Having agreed, McCririe's licence was renewed.

In April 1914 Greenall Whitley & Co. Ltd, brewers of St Helens, bought the Bear and Staff from the executors of the late Gateacre Brewery owner Thomas Gregory. Emily McCririe remained the licensee under the new owners until 16th November 1915 when John Kennedy took over the licence. Kennedy's stay at the inn was brief, and by June 1916 Samuel Holmes

Stirland had been granted the licence. Stirland provided a degree of stability to the house, and ran it until his death in 1927. Upon his death, his widow June Isabella Stirland became licensee. This was not for long, however, and in 1928 Alfred Beddell Grundy took over.

Less than a year later, Samuel James Scott, known simply as Sam Scott, held the licence, and ran the Bear and Staff without undue incident for a number of years. In 1936, however, Scott and one of his customers were at the centre of an illegal betting scandal at the inn. On 31st October 1936, a warrant was executed by the police at the premises, at this time being referred to as the Bear and Staff Hotel, and licensee Scott, along with a man called George Arthur Wilson, found themselves before the Liverpool Police Court on the 24th November.

It transpires that on the 21st October, and on several days afterwards, the Bear and Staff had been visited by plain clothes police officers. Giving evidence in court, Constable Buckle stated that at 1.10pm on the 21st, he entered the bar of the inn and saw Scott behind the counter. Also in the bar were several men and a woman, and one of the men was Wilson. One of the other men took a sporting paper from Wilson, looked at it, and said something to him. Wilson took out a blue notebook and wrote something in it, and the man gave something to Wilson who placed in in his pocket. It was alleged that another man called Wyke then entered the bar and had a discussion with Scott and Wilson about horse racing, before Wyke said, "I'll have a shilling each way, Generous Gift." Wilson again wrote in his notebook, and Wyke gave him something which he placed in his pocket. Wilson then said to Scott, "I'm going to ring them up now," whereupon Wilson entered the private kitchen of the hotel. A few moments later, Constable Buckle saw another man enter the bar who was dressed in clerical garb, and who was known as 'Brother John'. This male said something to Scott who replied, "Arthur is on the phone now," to which Brother John went into the news room of the hotel.

Constable Buckle gave further evidence of events on subsequent days. He alleged that on one occasion, after a plain clothes officer had left the hotel, licensee Scott said, "I don't know who that fellow is, but you want to be careful. We want no betting while he's in here in future. A licensee in Walton was done for the same thing."

On the day of the raid by police, the notebook belonging to Wilson was seized. The most recent page had been torn out, but ultra-violet light was used on the indentations of writing on the previous page. It was shown to relate to betting transactions, and written next to one of the transactions were the initials B.J.

In his defence, Sam Scott denied any involvement in illegal betting, or any knowledge that it was going on. He even denied being at the hotel when some of the incidents involving him were alleged to have taken place. Wilson also denied any involvement in betting in the Bear and Staff, claiming that betting notes found on his person were in relation to his own private bets, conducted at a bookmakers. The initials B.J. in his book related to his own brother, Joseph, and not Brother John. Despite his protestations, Scott was found guilty of permitting his premises to be used for betting and was fined £20 and costs. Wilson, from York Cottages in Gateacre, was also found guilty, and fined £5 plus costs.

Despite his conviction, Sam Scott remained as licensee of the Bear and Staff until 1939. The inn was run for a year by Frederick Vose, but in 1940 he was succeeded by Norman Lea.

The Bear and Staff survives to this day, and is one of the oldest surviving hostelries in the district. It is a popular pub and restaurant.

(Fig.43) The Bear and Staff on Gateacre Brow in 2020. The scene is still largely recognisable from how it was depicted over 200 years earlier.

THE PINFOLD HOUSE /
THE NEW INN /
THE BRIDGE INN

The Bridge Inn is closed and stands empty, and planning permission has been granted for its demolition and replacement with a retail store. The current structure was built in 1938 to replace the original inn which was much older. It stood on the ancient highway from Liverpool to Warrington which has been known by several names in the past including Pinfold lane, Tarbock Road, and Belle Vale Road. The road where the Bridge Inn currently stands is now part of the relatively modern Childwall Valley Road. There has been a house on the site for over 400 years, initially a Tudor era house and alehouse, built just in front of an area of land known as the Pinfold, and which became known as the Pinfold House.

First mention of the pinfold in Little Woolton can be found in the 16th century. In 1559, the township was ordered by the Manor Court of William Norris, to construct an '*abull pynfolde*' on the '*Le Grene*' or Lee Green. A pinfold is an area of land, fenced off and secured, which held cattle or livestock that was found to have strayed, or that had been seized by the town's bailiffs, and was waiting to be claimed by its owner on payment of a fee. The court's order came after Hugh Whitfield had broken into the existing pinfold to take a lamb which had been seized to pay a debt. It was therefore decided that the pinfold was inadequate and a better, more secure one was required.

The green which was to be the site of the pinfold was situated in an area between the Holt estate and the Lee. Centrally located within the township, the land was originally common land owned by the Lord of the Manor. The area was also the site of a major road junction which was the focal point for a small concentrated settlement consisting of a handful of alehouses, farmhouses and other dwellings. At this point the highway diverged and roads could be taken to Roby and Huyton, Warrington and Halewood, as well as access gained to the Holt and the Lee estates. There is also some indication that this was the original location of the town's stocks, conveniently located near to the Manor houses where the local courts were held. The pinfold enclosure itself was an area of meadow of just under two acres, and was opposite the old Bridge Lane, now called Naylor's Road, and just behind where the Bridge Inn currently stands.

The first mention of the house which was built in front of the pinfold was in 1622 when William and Ales Baxter surrendered the house, which they rented with three acres of land opposite known as the Dam Croft, to Henry Whitfield. The Dam Croft was so named as it lay against the stretch of Childwall Brook that had been diverted by a dam, the purpose of which was believed to have been to power a water mill once owned by the Knights Hospitallers. By this time the mill was long gone, but the fields surrounding what was known as 'the intake' from the brook still bore the names Dam Croft and Dam Meadow.

In 1628, Henry Whitfield died and his widow Marie continued to occupy the house, along with her son John. During their tenure as occupants of the house it became known locally as Whitfield House. At some point Marie began to operate the house as an alehouse, its position ideal for providing refreshment to travellers traversing the many routes that could be taken from that location.

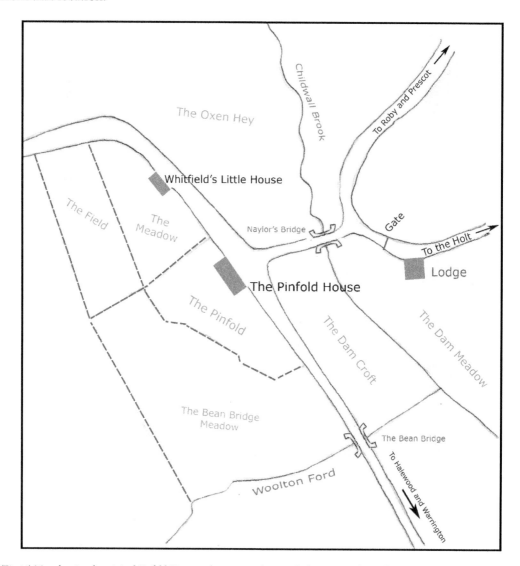

(Fig. 44) Map showing the original Pinfold House and its surroundings in the late 1600s. The Pinfold House was to become the New Inn, and later the Bridge Inn. Whitfield's Little House was to become the site of Jump's Cottages and the Halfway House beer house. The road both buildings stood on was the original road to Warrington, now part of Childwall Valley Road.

Marie Whitfield appears to have had a fairly uneventful time as an alehouse keeper, as she only appears once before the court for licensing offences. This was in 1635 when she failed to renew her alehouse licence and was fined 2 shillings. Whitfield avoids being before the court again until October 1649, when she permitted Henry Whitfield, her nephew, to take up residence at her house, and to begin running the inn. His occupancy did not find favour with the manor court, and neither did his conduct as a licensee. Henry Whitfield found himself before the court for breaches of the licensing laws, when he was summoned for keeping unlawful gaming in the house. It appears that several persons had been caught 'gaming for cakes' at an unlawful time of the night. They were James Orme, Thomas Orme, John Lyon of Much Woolton, William Bradshall, Richard Catton of Halewood, James Whitfield, Henry Mowas, Ellin Harrison, William and Elizabeth Highfield, and two men called Henry Gorsuch and Thomas Lawrie who were described as 'servants to Mr Brettargh', owner of the Holt estate. At the same court Marie Whitfield was presented for taking Henry Whitfield as an 'inmake' or resident of her house without due consent of the officers of the manor, and was fined 3 shillings and 4 pence. She was also ordered to remove Henry Whitfield, his wife and children, before the first of May 1650 on pain of 40 shillings. Needless to say, this is the last time Henry Whitfield appears to have been engaged as an alehouse keeper within the township.

By 1654, Marie Whitfield was dead, and Whitfield's House came into the possession of Henry Whitfield, her grandson. In 1658, the house was referred to as the Pinfold House for the first time, and was owned by James Brettargh of the Holt, though the Whitfields were still its long standing tenants. The copyhold passed down from Henry Whitfield to his son John.

The Pinfold House remained in the possession of the Whitfield family, though occupied by a series of under tenants, for the next 40 years. There is no evidence that the house was an alehouse during this period until, in 1686, alehouse keeper Henry Halewood became the tenant of the house. The Halewood family had, for many years, run several alehouses on Grange Lane. In 1694, Henry Halewood acquired the full copyhold to the Pinfold House, paying £30 to John Whitfield. The same year the town's aletasters had been admonished by the manorial court for failing to bring in any presentments for the preceding few years, so Halewood found himself being presented for '*the breach of ye measure of ale*.' Halewood was fined for assize of ale offences every year until 1699, after which all presentments for licensing offences stop. Halewood remained the occupant of the Pinfold House for a number of years, though the actual ownership of the premises often changed. In 1701, James Brettargh of the Holt surrendered the copyhold for the Pinfold House to Ralph Markland who was the vicar of Childwall. However, in 1705 Henry Halewood bought back the copyhold for £32, and also had to pay 3s 1d per year to the Lady of the Manor and 3s 1d per year to James Brettargh. He also had to perform a day's reaping of corn for Brettargh at harvest time, and to keep and maintain for Brettargh one dog.

Henry Halewood's death was reported at the manorial court of April 1711, having occurred the previous February. His widow Ellen was left to run the inn, until she herself died in 1727. The copyhold for the property was sold by her son John Halewood to John Bispham. Shortly afterwards, in 1730, it was acquired by Peter Ellam, an apothecary from Chester, though Bispham remained as tenant. In 1767, the house and land was acquired by John Okill of the Lee, and was incorporated into his ever expanding estate.

Following the Halewood family's tenure at the Pinfold House there is no evidence that it remained a tavern. Certainly by 1753 it was not shown as licenced. Over the years that followed, the Pinfold House underwent a number of changes, most notably being extended into two dwellings and being referred to as Pinfold Houses. In the 1841 census, the Pinfold Houses are shown being occupied by the families of Joseph Hunter and William Nichols. By 1848 the Pinfold itself had long fallen out of use, though it was still referred to as the Pinfold Meadow.

The Houses remained as part of Okill's Lee estate, and in the 1860s were in the occupation of gardener Frederick Guy. Guy converted the two Pinfold Houses back into a single dwelling and, in 1866, he applied to the court for a liquor license. Its location and prior history as an alehouse made it an ideal prospect for Guy to re-open it as such. The house was described as having nine rooms, and Guy promised, if successful in his application, to make some minor improvements to the premises. He also stated his intention to give up his occupation as gardener to run the house full time. The license was granted. Guy became a licensed victualler, and his tavern became the 'New Inn'. The area behind the inn which had been the old Little Woolton pinfold, became the inn's gardens and bowling green.

(Fig.45) The Bridge Inn in 2019 closed and awaiting demolition, as viewed from the original Naylor's Road and the remains of the old Naylor's Bridge from which the inn took its name © Stuart Rimmer

Guy ran the inn for only six years, and in 1872 decided to call an end to his time as an innkeeper. He put all his effects up for sale at auction, and returned to plying his trade as a gardener.

In 1873, the New Inn was being run by Joseph Ratcliffe, an experienced victualler originally from Chorley. It was under Ratcliffe that the inn's name was changed to the 'Bridge Inn', after Naylor's Bridge which was situated opposite the building, a few hundred yards along the original Naylor's Lane. In 1880, the inn, which was in the hands of the executors of the late owner Thomas Dutton, was offered for sale by auction, however the reserve price was not met and ultimately the lot was withdrawn. That year, Ratcliffe died and the licence was granted to his wife Eliza, who ran it for a short time, until in December 1881 John Poole became the licensee. In 1882, the Bridge Inn was briefly owned by John Scales, who also bought the Lee estate, however the deal fell through and the inn ended back in the hands of Dutton's executors, with whom it remained for many years afterwards. John Poole remained the licensee until the end of the century, and his tenure was not without incident.

On 4th March 1889, Poole appeared at Woolton court accused of selling sub-standard whiskey. Some weeks earlier, on 29th January, Inspector Webb of the weights and measures department of the Woolton Police had attended the Bridge Inn, and had sent a 10 year old boy named Taylor into the house to obtain 2 shillings' worth of Irish whiskey. The Inspector met the boy at the door as he was coming out of the inn, and then took the purchased whisky back to Poole telling him it had been obtained for the purpose of analysis. When it was analysed it was found to be 5% less proof than it should have been by law, and Poole was summonsed to court. At the hearing Poole was represented by lawyer Mr Edwin Berry. Berry was one of the lawyers of the period who was considered an expert in licensing law, and was often employed by breweries and licensees to defend them in court. The defences Berry and his ilk put forward were often convoluted and complex, to reflect their perceived expertise. They were also conceived to outsmart the prosecuting police superintendent, as well as impress and even confuse the magistrates and throw some doubt on the evidence in the case. This approach was sometimes successful, and other times not. On this occasion Mr Berry's defence of Poole was based upon a scientific technicality. Berry argued that a vent peg had inadvertently come out of the whisky cask, and that there was also a hole in the bottle used to dispense the alcohol to customers. Berry argued that these two factors had caused some evaporation of the alcohol from the two vessels, thereby reducing its concentration, and resulting in Poole unintentionally supplying weak whisky. The court were having none of it and dismissed the defence's explanation, choosing to believe that Poole was quite simply watering down his whiskey. He was fined 5 shillings for the offence and 32 shillings costs.

On 1st July 1891, John Poole was host to an excursion of 43 of the principal tradespeople of the village of Ashton in Makerfield, who had made the journey with the intention of spending the day using the bowling green at the inn, and enjoying the outdoor areas of the premises. Unfortunately, the heavens opened, forcing the party to take shelter in the inn, which was described as 'scarcely capable of inwardly entertaining so large a company'.

On 15th January 1897, John Poole appeared at the Woolton courthouse charged with permitting gaming at the Bridge Inn, an offence which could see the licensee fined as much as £10 if found guilty. What followed at the trial was an examination of the law in respect of gaming, and whether in this instance it had been broken. Gaming has long been described in law as the playing of a game of chance, or chance and skill combined, for money or money's worth.

Prosecuting the case for the police was Superintendent Baxendale, while lawyer Edwin Berry defended. The circumstances were that on the evening of 19th December 1896, two plain clothes officers – constables William Martin and George Hill – entered the tap room of the inn. They had had not been there long when four men came in and two of them agreed to play each other at a game of rings, or 'parlour quoits'. They agreed to play for beer. The two men played for a while, but had to leave to catch a train before they could finish. Then the licensee, Poole, entered the room and said to two other men, "Slavin, you can beat Dennett." At that, the two men agreed to play each other for drinks, and commenced a game. Dennett won the game, and Slavin bought him a beer. The men played again, and again Slavin lost and bought Dennett a beer.

Superintendent Baxendale addressed the magistrates, explaining that in previous cases, playing skittles for beer had been held to be 'gaming' under the act, and that parlour quoits being a game of chance…

"Skill." Immediately interjected Mr Berry.

Superintendent Baxendale looked at him, and then back to the magistrates, saying "that is for your worships to decide."

Mr Berry then said, "I don't think there will be any dispute regarding the law." Berry's inference was that it was not the law concerning the act of gaming that was up for debate, rather the nature of the game being played. The lawyer further posited that even if the playing of parlour quoits *could* be held to be gaming, which he maintained it wasn't, it was perfectly lawful unless it was played for money or money's worth, which was yet to be proven.

Constable Hill gave evidence to the fact that he believed that quoits, when played for beer, was an offence and that he had been sent to the house to specifically look for gaming. Mr Berry questioned as to why, if the police knew that so called gaming was taking place at the Bridge Inn, did they not seek to alert the licensee to the fact, thus alleviating the need for such a trivial matter to come before the court? Another point which must be proven was that Poole had knowingly 'suffered' the gaming to take place. Constable Martin testified that Poole was present when the men played the game, and also when they agreed to play for beer. Mr Berry argued that Poole had acquired the rings only a few weeks previously after requests from some of his customers. He did not know that they were playing for anything other than the love of the game.

Poole denied knowing the men were playing for beer. Both Charles Dennett, a Gateacre gardener, and Thomas Slavin, who was unemployed, gave evidence to state they did not agree to play for beer, and that Slavin only paid for Dennett's drinks because he was out of work and short of money. On this occasion Edwin Berry's defence was successful and the magistrates threw the case out.

Despite Poole's innocence in the eyes of the law, the Trustees of the late Thomas Sutton, owners of the Bridge Inn, decided to give Poole notice to quit, citing their desire to accept 'an altogether better offer' for the tenancy of the public house. Poole, however, was not willing to relinquish his tenancy so easily, and mounted a legal challenge based chiefly on the grounds that the written notice sent to him was not legally valid. What followed was a period of discussions between the solicitors of the parties involved until, in April 1899, a final and legally correct written notice was served on Poole requiring him to quit the Bridge Inn by November 1st that year.

In September 1899, at the licensing sessions held at Woolton Court, the local police made some objections regarding the premises of the Bridge Inn. Superintendent Baxendale stated that the boundary of the inn was not properly defined, and the bowling green at the rear opened onto a field where the licensee held tea parties and served liquor in the summer months. The court adjourned the hearing to allow the licensee to suggest a remedy to the situation. At the adjourned hearing in October, Mr Swift, the lawyer represented the Bridge Inn, stated that the owner was willing to build a fence at the rear of the premises to fully enclose them, and to build a wall at the front to define where the premises of the inn was separate from the road. There was also an undertaking from the licensee that intoxicants would only be served within recognised boundaries of the premises, and that serving liquor on the field at the rear would cease. The proposed alterations found favour with the Police. However, before the licence was renewed, the Chairman of the bench raised another issue. He stated that he had himself visited the Bridge Inn, and that on the occasion of his visit the brook that ran beneath Naylor's Bridge was in flood and that the waters were unsanitary, causing a foul smell about the inn. He wished this to be attended to for the sake of public welfare. Licensee Poole stated that it was a problem, and it also affected his health, but that it was a difficult situation to resolve as there was nowhere for the water to be drained away. Mr Swift assured the bench that a solution would be sought, and the licence was renewed. Whether a solution to the flooding problem was ever found at that time is not clear, but the issue does not appear to have been raised again.

Having been required to move on, Poole placed all his inn keeper's effects up for auction. Poole's effects, fixtures and fittings were purchase for £130 by George Marples Freeman, originally from Retford in Nottinghamshire, who had previously been a publican in Hull. He had more recently been employed as a painter, living in Smithdown Road in Liverpool, and had lived in Widnes prior to that. Freeman took out a five year lease on the Bridge Inn, and on 3rd November 1899 he attended the Woolton Court to apply for temporary transfer of the licence. Due to a technicality, the magistrates sitting that day could not adjudicate on licensing matters, resulting in the Freeman's licensing application being delayed. As a consequence the Bridge Inn had to close its doors until 17th November, when Freeman again attended court to apply for transfer of the license. During the hearing, Superintendent Baxendale posed some questions to Freeman which tended to suggest that the police had received some less than favourable intelligence about the prospective licensee. The superintendent asked Freeman if he had any connections with betting, and specifically with running some kind of betting operation when in Widnes. Freeman categorically denied this, supported by his lawyer. After making a promise to give up his painting business to run the inn full time, he was granted the licence.

Freeman, however, was not at the Bridge Inn long. On 19th October 1900, Freeman's wife, Mary Elizabeth, attended Woolton Court to ask for transfer of the licence. It seems that Freeman had gotten himself into unspecified financial difficulties, and had quit the premises. He had not been at the Bridge Inn for two weeks and did not intend to return. Mrs Freeman's lawyer, Mr S. Taylor Dixon, told the court that Mrs Freeman had experience in the licensing trade, having held two licences in Hull and knew the business well. Superintendent Baxendale opposed the transfer, stating that the circumstances were wholly unsatisfactory, and as licensee George Freeman had responsibilities which he couldn't just run away from. The bench were inclined to agree and refused the transfer.

It appears that the Bridge Inn was losing money, and consequently George Freeman had found himself deeply in debt. He had ultimately fled the premises leaving his wife and family behind, with Mary trying to pick up the pieces by applying for the licence. By November it was clear that the Freemans could not continue running the house, and the family left. George Freeman returned to Hull with his eldest son to live with his mother. The rest of the family remained in Little Woolton, living with Mary's mother. On 16th November 1900 Robert Ryley from Widnes applied for transfer of the licence for the inn, having taken over the lease. This was approved, and on the 1st February 1901, Ryley was granted full transfer of the licence.

Ryley moved to the Bridge Inn with his wife, Mary and their daughter. He ran the inn it seems without real incident, until he fell ill in 1906. On 30th October, with Ryley's his health failing, Thomas Lewis, a barman employed at the premises, applied for a temporary license to run the inn as a stop gap until Ryley recovered. Sadly Ryley died on 19th November 1906, aged only 37 years. Following his death, the licence was transferred to his widow Mary. The Bridge Inn was run by Mary Ryley for another year and on 21st November 1907 the licence was transferred to Joseph Wilson. After four years in charge, the licence was transferred from Joseph Wilson to his son, Joseph Wilson junior, on 3rd February 1911.

(Fig.46) The original Bridge Inn around 1912 and the licensee at the time Joseph Wilson jnr.

In 1914, at the first licensing sessions since the incorporation of Little Woolton into the city of Liverpool, Wilson had to give an undertaking that he would cease serving intoxicating liquor on the bowling green, as seemed to be the practice at many of the pubs in the area. In 1917, the Bridge Inn was bought from the trustees of the late Thomas Dutton by Higson's Brewery. Wilson ran the Bridge Inn until 1924, when the licence was transferred to Alfred Rudolph Tennant. Tennant was licensee until 1929, when he was replaced by a new licensee in the person of Edward Hall.

Higson's, who also owned the nearby Halfway House beer house, had big plans for the Bridge Inn. In January 1936, Higson's applied to the Liverpool Magistrates for permission to build new, larger premises to replace the old inn. The brewery had employed architects H.H. & H.E. Davies from Liverpool, and stated their intention was to construct a premises which was seven times larger than the old building. It was to be set back 60 yards from the roadway and would accommodate motor cars, which would be able to drive in and out and be provided ample parking space. The accommodation would include a large dining room and tea rooms and a pavilion near the bowling green. It was argued that there would be plenty of custom for the proposed inn, as the new Childwall Valley Road was quite busy with traffic. There were also 1,170 new houses planned for the area, and it was anticipated that, on a fine summer Saturday afternoon, up to 500 customers could be accommodated at the rebuilt inn. In an effort to influence the court's decision, Higson's offered to surrender the licence of the nearby Halfway House beer house should the plans be approved[1]. The building of a new inn was challenged by a Gateacre residents' group who argued that there was currently no demand for a public house of the size suggested, and that it should not be built on mere supposition of such demand in the future. The bench were inclined to agree and the plans were rejected.

In September 1936, Higson's made another attempt to have plans for rebuilding the Bridge Inn approved. The plans had been revised, and whereas the previous plans had sought an increase to the floor space of 554 square yards, the new plans proposed an increase of only 125 square yards. This was an expansion of the current premises of only half as much again, rather than the seven times larger previously applied for. Lawyer R.K. Milne, acting for Higson's, stated that the current inn was very old and inadequate, leading to a great deal of congestion at the weekends. Licensee Edward Hall gave evidence that one of his customers had said to him, "in the summer you can't get in, and in the winter you can't stay in – it's too uncomfortable." Mr Milne argued that, in contrast to the previous application, the current proposals catered for current demand, and not for the future. Mr S.E. Dodds spoke for the Gateacre residents who opposed the building of a new inn. An argument was made that the population of Gateacre was only 300 people, and there were already three other public houses in the area. Very few people lived within half a mile of the Bridge Inn, so the demand did not exist. The counter argument from Mr Milne was that the figures clearly showed there was a demand, and that the appeal of a country inn was not limited to local residents only, but to visitors and travellers through the area. If country inns were licensed solely on local demand then they wouldn't exist at all. Once again, the court found against Higson's and the plans were not approved.

(Fig.47) Photograph from 1938 showing the new Bridge Inn on the left standing next to the old Bridge Inn on the right, shortly before the latter's demolition

Higson's were not to be denied. In 1937, another effort to have the plans approved, along the same lines as in September 1936, was successful. The building of a new, only moderately larger, Bridge Inn commenced. The premises were constructed alongside the old building, and built very much in the style of the original 17th century house, a fact Higson's made mention of in subsequent promotions. Shortly before the completion of the rebuilt inn, the old building was demolished, though for a time the old and new stood side by side. The new public house was open for business by July 1938, with a new licensee in Ronald Lawson Steele. As promised in their application, Higson's surrendered the licence of the Halfway House, which stood just over a hundred yards away, and the old beer house ceased trading.

Ronald Steele lasted only a year as the licensee of the new Bridge Inn, and in 1939 he was replaced by James Millard. Millard ran the Bridge Inn through the Second World War, and the inn remained in business for the rest of the 20th century and into the 21st. The pub closed its doors in 2016 and is currently awaiting demolition.

[1]Surprisingly, a factor which did not appear to have been raised in court, and which may have strengthened the Brewery's case, was the fact that the construction of a major new outer ring road was being planned as part of the Liverpool Town Planning Scheme No. 2. The 120 foot wide boulevard was intended to intersect Childwall Valley Road before heading on to Widnes, and could have been used to justify the building of a new large hotel on the site of the Bridge Inn. As it happens the scheme was never completed. The construction of Kings Drive was as far as development got in that area before being abandoned.

(Fig.48) Higson's Brewery advert from July 1938.
The new Bridge Inn was built very much in the style of the 17th century original.

NOW OPEN!
The BRIDGE INN
GATEACRE

Originally a little wayside Inn, built over two hundred years ago—now a magnificent Hotel! But the new Bridge Inn clings to its memories of the past. It is what the original might have looked like had the builders of bygone days used the choice woods and lovely decorative materials that are at hand to-day. You must come to Gateacre and see for yourself the charming old-world atmosphere created for your pleasure. The Garden Hall is considered one of the finest reproductions of the Tudor style in the country, while on a Summer's day or evening the view from the Terrace across pleasant countryside well repays the visit. There is a Bowling Green and large Car Park for patrons, and with these and all its other amenities the Bridge Inn is certain to become a popular rendezvous with Merseysiders.

View of the Bridge Inn from the bowling green, showing the terrace and lily pond.

Best of all it's a
HIGSON'S HOTEL

THE HALFWAY HOUSE

(Fig.49) Licensee Sarah Greig with three of her children outside the Halfway House beer house in around 1899, just before alterations were made by owner Colonel William Hall Walker. The beer house takes up most of the row with two entrances and enlarged ground floor windows. Photo used with kind permission of the Gateacre Society.

The 'Halfway House' was a beer house which was situated just a couple of hundred yards from the Bridge Inn. It has been demolished and is now long gone. The old house that became the original beer house was one of a row of small cottages, once known as Jump's Cottages, which stood near to what is now the junction of Belle Vale Road and Childwall Valley Road. Before the new Childwall valley Road was constructed in the 20th century, there was no junction at this location, rather it was a bend in the road where it changed its course to lead south towards Halewood and Warrington.

The area of land on the south west side of this bend was enclosed from the commons in the early 17th century by the owner of the Lee estate, Thomas Orme. After his death the area, which was two parcels of land known as The Meadow and The Field, was acquired by John Cooke, who owned by copyhold much of the land and property bordering with the Lee estate. First mention of a dwelling on the land was in 1642, when Cooke let the land, along with a house and yard, to tailor John Knowles, his wife Jane and daughter Elizabeth. The Knowles family were tenants under Cooke for a number of years. In 1661 the land, described as 'near the pinfold' was acquired by Richard Orme of the Grange. John Knowles continued to occupy the property until it came into the ownership of blacksmith John Whitfield in 1680.

The land and house near the pinfold, which was also referred to as the 'Little House', was owned by the Whitfield family until 1708, when it was bought by Jonathan Case. Despite having surrendered the property to Case, the Whitfields continued as occupiers. In 1738, upon Jonathan Case's death, it passed to his son and heir Thomas Case. However, by 1740 Case had sold the property to Richard Jump.

The small estate remained in the ownership of Richard Jump, and then his son Henry, for over 50 years. During this time the house had been rebuilt and expanded to incorporate 3 dwellings, and in 1792 the three dwellings were sold by Jump to Thomas Molyneux. The field at the rear, referred to by this time as 'Jump's Meadow', was purchased by Thurston Pinnington. Molyneux added a fourth cottage to the row of houses, known as 'Jump's Houses' and, eventually, he purchased Jump's Meadow also.

The Beer House Act of 1830 had provided an opportunity for the occupiers of any property, regardless of how small, to operate it as a beer house. Around 1840, farmer Robert Roberts, originally from Wrexham, rented one of the cottages, and the field at the rear, from the executors of the late Thomas Molyneux. Roberts, who lived at the house with his wife Betsy and their children, obtained a beer license and opened his house as a beer house, which became known as the Halfway House.

At the Woolton licensing sessions on 5th September 1862, Roberts applied for a full liquor license for the premises. The magistrates considered the house, which Roberts rented for £14 per year, as too small and inadequate. Despite lawyer Starling Worship making arguments in support of the application it was refused. Roberts continued to operate his beer house until his death in 1867 when the license was taken on by his widow Betsy. On 4th September 1868, at the court sitting at the Woolton Mechanic's Institute, Betsy Roberts was fined 5 shillings plus 12 shillings costs for keeping her house open during prohibited hours.

Betsy Roberts ran the small beer house until 1873, when the license was acquired by 62-year-old George Houghton, a wheelwright by trade who was also an experienced beer house licensee[1]. Houghton kept the house for ten years until, in 1883, he was succeeded as licensee by James Harris. By this time, the Halfway House had been expanded to incorporate another of the small cottages.

In 1888 Harris was involved in an incident which could have turned out far worse for him than it did. On the 14th September that year, Harris was in Wavertree High Street, sitting in his horse and trap, when he became involved in an altercation with Wavertree butcher James Doran. A witness at the time had seen Doran, who it was claimed was drunk at the time, walk up to where Harris was sitting. The witness believed Doran was about to shake Harris' hand, when Harris either struck or pushed Doran who fell to the ground and hit his head. The unconscious Doran was taken to the nearby Lamb Inn and the police were called. Doran died the next morning. Harris was arrested, and when questioned by the police stated that he had argued with a drunken Doran, but could not recall whether he had struck Doran or not. He was released on bail with a £50 surety, half of which was stood by Alexander Martin, the licensee of the Bull Inn in Gateacre. An inquest into Doran's death, held at Wavertree Town Hall, returned a verdict of death by misadventure. In the light of the jury's conclusion,

Inspector Peter of the Wavertree Police declined to offer any further evidence against Harris and he was acquitted.

James Harris ran the Halfway House until his death in 1892 and the licence was transferred to his wife Susannah. On 6th December 1895, Susannah Harris appeared in court charged with selling drink on a Sunday during prohibited hours. The case raised the 'bona fide traveller' issue, an aspect of 19th century licensing law that was frequently the focus of debate in the courts of the time. The licensing laws of the late 19th century allowed a person who was deemed to be making a journey of a reasonable distance, generally understood to be of 3 miles or more, and who had developed a thirst, to call at a licensed house and purchase alcoholic refreshment outside of permitted licensing hours. But the bona fide traveller question posed difficulties for the authorities. It was often no easy task for the police to determine who was a bona fide traveller, and whether any offences had been committed. The courts were left with the task of examining the evidence and making a decision on the guilt or otherwise of the parties involved.

The circumstances that led to licensee Harris being before the Woolton court were that at 5pm on Sunday 17th November, PC Taylor visited the Halfway House to find eight men inside with beer in front of them. He recognised two of the men as being from Woolton, less than two miles away. One of them was called William Carroll, and the other Edward Carroll, who was wearing a soldier's uniform. When the constable questioned licensee Harris about the men she stated that they had told her they were from Wavertree, which would have fallen outside of the three mile limit. The other men present were from Liverpool and Prescot. The two Woolton men and the licensee were then summonsed by the officer to appear at court. At the hearing, Superintendent Baxendale, who was prosecuting, described the Halfway House as a very small beer house, which was hardly likely to attract anyone other than those wishing to drink. Susannah Harris felt her defence was on shaky ground, and therefore pleaded guilty to serving beer during prohibited hours. The two Woolton men were also found guilty on the evidence provided. They were all fined 10 shillings and costs.

On 21st August 1896, when Susannah Harris appeared in court to have her beer licence renewed, the Police objected to the renewal on the grounds of her conviction some months earlier. However, Mr Knowles, the lawyer for Harris, made the case that there had been no disorder involved. As the Halfway House was a pre-1869 'privileged' house, with a licence issued by the excise, the powers of the court were somewhat restricted. For the court to refuse renewal of the licence, the house had to be proven to be a disorderly one, which it was not. The magistrates therefore renewed the licence.

On 2nd July 1897, Susannah Harris again appeared before the Woolton Magistrates charged with permitting drunkenness in her house, and supplying liquor to a drunken man. On the evening of 19th June, PC Taylor had attended the house and found a man named Sparks on the premises in a state of intoxication. The lawyer for the licensee, Mr Knowles, did not deny that Sparks was drunk, but called Harris and two other witnesses who had been in the house at the time to testify that Sparks had only just entered the house before the constable arrived and had not been served with any beer. The magistrates accepted this explanation and the case against Harris was withdrawn. Sparks, however was fined 5 shillings and costs for being drunk whilst on licensed premises.

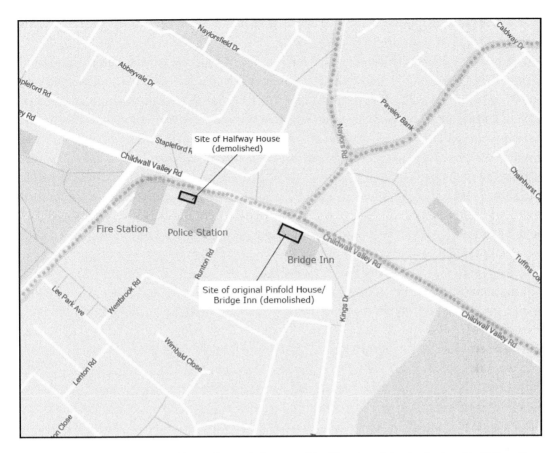

(Fig.50) A modern map with the dotted lines indicating the locations of the old roads, and showing the sites of the Halfway House and the original Bridge Inn, both of which are now demolished.

Susannah Harris kept the beer house until late 1897 when it was taken over by cowman John Greig, originally from Ireland, and his wife Sarah from Halewood. At the same time the Halfway House and attached cottages were bought by Colonel William Hall Walker, who lived at Gateacre Grange in Rose Brow. On 5th April 1899, John Grieg died aged only 41 years, and on 21st April Sarah Greig was granted a license to take over from her late husband.

At the annual licensing sessions held at Woolton Court on 25th August 1899, the police objected to the licence renewal for the Halfway House. The beer house, they claimed was small, in a bad state of repair and in an unsanitary condition. The hearing for the licence renewal was adjourned to allow the owner Colonel Walker to come up with a solution. At the adjourned hearing on 29th September, a plan was submitted to the court by architect W.H. Jones. The proposal was to knock the beer house through into the cottage next door, and to convert the new area into a kitchen. The current kitchen, which was also used as a sitting room, would become a smoke room. The windows at the front of the house would be enlarged to give the house a better overall appearance, and the end gable wall would be rebuilt. The plans were approved and the licence renewal granted. By 1900 the Halfway House had been expanded to incorporate all of the small cottages. It had also been provided with a mock Tudor appearance typical of renovations carried out by the Walker family to their other licensed houses in the area, such as the Black Bull and, a few years later, the Brown Cow. The larger cottage on the end of the row, itself formerly two cottages, remained separate from the beer house and at that time was occupied by farm labourer Richard Ashley.

On Sunday 2nd March 1902 at 4.30pm, which was outside of permitted licensing hours, three men entered the Halfway House stating they had travelled from Garston, just beyond the three-mile limit. They were William Humphreys and William Henry Jackson from Mason Street, Woolton and Edward Jolley from Garston, all of the men employed as boilermakers. The men asked for two pints of beer and a lemonade, which they were served by the licensee's daughter, Mary Elizabeth Greig. Ten minutes later they asked for a second round, and after serving them, Mary momentarily left them and went into the kitchen. When she returned to the bar, she saw Humphreys leaving the area of the counter with two bottles of stout which he was putting into his coat pockets. As he left the house, Mary heard one of the other men ask Humphreys if he had been caught, to which he replied, "I think she has seen me." The men made off, and PC Carlton, who was in the area, was alerted. The men had made it as far as the top of Out Lane, near to the Elephant Hotel, before the constable had caught up with them. He stopped the men and found four bottles of stout in the coat pockets of Humphreys and Jackson. The men were arrested and, denying they had stolen the beer, were remanded for trial at Woolton Court on 7th March. At the hearing both Humphreys and Jackson admitted theft, but Jolley denied having anything to do with it. In his defence Jolley stated that he had accepted an invitation from the other two men to go for a walk. He therefore went from Garston to Woolton, and then the three of them walked around Lee Hall. When they got to the Halfway House the other two wanted a drink, but Jolley, being teetotal, just a had a couple of bottles of lemonade. When Humphreys and Jackson said they wanted a third pint, Jolley claimed he told them he'd had enough and went to wait for them outside. It was a short time later that they appeared carrying the bottles of stout. Jolley asked them how they had come by them and they told him that they had just taken them. Jolley told the court that he had advised his friends to take the bottles back or pay for them, but they refused to do so. Jackson and Humphreys were called as witnesses for Jolley and corroborated his story. The chairman of the bench told Jolley that his actions had perhaps not been as honourable as he would like them to appear, as he had known the bottles were stolen but had kept the fact to himself. However he stated the bench would give him the benefit of the doubt and dismissed the case against him. As well as the theft, Humphreys and Jackson were charged with falsely representing themselves as travellers. The fastidious Sgt Elsworth of the Woolton police had measured the distance from the Halfway House to the homes of the Woolton men, and found it to be 1 mile and 876 yards. In response Jackson stated that they walked the long way round, believing that if they at least walked the required distance they were entitled to a drink. The two men were fined 20 shillings for each offence plus costs.

In February 1903 the Halfway House was one of many beer houses inspected by the Licensing Justices as part of the annual renewal hearings. Whereas many of the other establishments in the district had been found wanting in some way, Sarah Greig's house was found to be in a relatively acceptable condition, with only minor alterations needed to satisfy the court. The license was renewed with little objection.

Sarah Greig was licensee of the Halfway House until 1910, when the licence was transferred to John Shacklady. Shacklady and his wife Margaret, along with servant Mary Brady, took occupation of the beer house, but were resident for less than three years. On 6th February 1913, at the annual licensing sessions, the licence was transferred to Arthur Paulson. Paulson had been a barman in Bradford before taking over at the Gateacre beer house. He was in charge of the Halfway House for less than a year, and in January 1914 the licence was taken on by Edward Cowley.

In 1917 William Hall Walker's Gateacre Grange estate and other holdings in Little Woolton were sold to Edgar Creyke Fairweather of Kingswear, Devon, and in October 1917, the numerous properties, including the Halfway House beer house, were put up for sale by auction. Despite this, it appears from licensing records that the house was not actually sold until much later when it was purchased by Joseph Jones' Brewery of Knotty Ash.

Edward Cowley ran the Halfway House until 1927, when Albert Edward Sporage took over running the house for a further year. In 1928 the house had a new licensee in Thomas McCormack, though he lasted less than a year, being replaced in June 1929 by Henry Roe. In August 1929, Joseph Jones & Co. of Knotty Ash sent a letter to the Liverpool licensing authorities informing them they had taken ownership of the beer house, though Joseph Jones & Co. were themselves owned by Higson's Brewery[2].

Taking over from Roe, Lilian Edey ran the beer house in 1934 and 1935, and in 1936 the licence was held by James Leonard Bailey, who was to be the last licensee of the Halfway House. Higson's wished to demolish the nearby Bridge Inn, which they also owned, intending to build a new, bigger hotel in its place. When they submitted the first application for a new Bridge Inn to the licensing court in 1936, they offered to surrender the licence of the Halfway House in order to encourage the bench to approve their plans. This was to no avail, as the court saw no need for a new hotel in the area and rejected the application. Higson's were not to be outdone, and submitted several more applications in the preceding months. Eventually, the plans were approved on the proviso that the licence for Halfway House be given up.

In 1938 the rebuilt Bridge Inn was ready to open and, after a century as a beer house, the Halfway House was no more. It became a confectioners and general store run by William Crosby. Being unnumbered, it retained the address 'Halfway House' for several years afterwards, but its days as a licensed house were over.

The old block of cottages was eventually demolished to make way for the police station and fire station which stand on the site today.

(Fig.51) A watercolour by Alfred H. Jones depicting the former Halfway House beer house in 1948, with the mock Tudor appearance it was given by William Hall Walker at the turn of the century. Used with permission of Liverpool Record Office, Liverpool Libraries.

Notes:

[1] For many years George Houghton had been in charge of the Folly Vale Tavern, a beer house on Folly Vale Lane near Woolton. He had been forced to give up his license in 1869 when the beer house was demolished to allow for the building of a mansion house for merchant Robert Gladstone which was called Woolton Vale. After a spell running the Old House at Home beer house in Woolton, and a couple of years on Quarry Street as a wheelwright, Houghton returned to licensing and took over the Halfway House.

[2] In October 1927, Higson's Brewery became a majority shareholder in Joseph Jones & Co. of Knotty Ash, buying the shares belonging to the directors of the company. The directors were then re-employed by Higson's at a salary of £1000 each per annum to continue to run Joseph Jones & Co. as a going concern. Although brewing ceased at Knotty Ash in 1928, Joseph Jones & Co. continued on as a company, and was not dissolved until 1948.

JOHN BLACKBURN'S / THE RAILWAY

(Fig.52) Top: Number 1 Stone Cottages on Belle vale Road, Gateacre, was once John Blackburn's beer house, later called the Railway Inn. The wooden window surround dates from its time as a public house. Bottom: Holes in the stone above the door shows where the sign would have been affixed.

The beer house that became known as John Blackburn's was one of a row of stone cottages that still stand on Belle Vale Road, near to the junction with Halewood Road, at the Gateacre crossroads.

Prior to the early 19th century, the land upon which the cottages were built was two separate open fields known as Holmes Hey, and Holmes Meadow. In the early 1800s the land was owned by lawyer Joshua Lace, and in 1837 a local family of stonemasons, the Greenoughs, took an interest in it. In October 1837, John Greenough purchased part of the land from Lace, and other members of the Greenough family made an agreement to purchase the adjoining plots. The building of the cottages commenced, but Joshua Lace died before the purchase of the all of the land by the various members of the Greenough family could be finalised. It wasn't until 1842 that the Greenoughs managed to finally complete the deal with Joshua Lace's son and heir Ambrose Lace, and the building of the row known as Sandstone Cottages was finished.

Owner of the first small stone cottage in the row, set back from the road by its garden, and next to the more prominent corner house, was Richard Greenough. Richard was a friend and acquaintance of Halewood Brewery owner Isaac Moss, and so it's no surprise that he opened his house as a beer house selling Halewood Ale. In March 1844 Richard Greenough, who had been a widower for some years, died and was buried at Childwall Church. His brother William Greenough, and brewer Isaac Moss, were made his executors, and William was appointed as guardian of Richard's four children. Instruction was also given that, if need be, his house and property were to be sold to provide for his children's education, however it appears William Greenough acquired the house himself, and proceeded to run the beer house into the 1850s.

Sometime after 1862, the beer house was taken over by butcher John Blackburn. Blackburn was the son of a Woolton butcher, and had been born on Woolton Street in 1840. In 1862 had married Martha Radley, daughter of Liverpool brewer William Radley. Blackburn and his new wife moved to Gateacre and he ran the beer house on Belle Vale Road for the next four decades. The house simply became known as 'John Blackburn's'. Although he was a licensee, Blackburn did not relinquish the family trade, and also operated a butchers shop just around the corner on Halewood Road. He kept livestock, and occasionally grazed his sheep on the nearby Gateacre recreation grounds, to the consternation of the Little Woolton Local Board.

In general it appears John Blackburn ran an orderly and well-kept house, and very rarely came before the courts for licensing matters. However, one occasion when he did was on 6th February 1903, when Blackburn's beer licence was due for renewal at the Woolton Court on Quarry Street. Along with the other beer houses in both Much and Little Woolton, the renewal hearing was adjourned to allow the magistrates to personally inspect Blackburne's house for themselves.

On 13th March the adjourned licensing sessions took place, and the bench took issue with the condition of John Blackburn's house. The sanitary condition of the premises was described as most unsuitable, with the state of the urinals and the access to them being a particular issue. The only route to the urinals for patrons was through the private kitchen, and the premises was described as being in a filthy state. The public area was small and inadequate, and the back door to the yard was kept unlocked, allowing unsupervised access to the house from the rear. The bench renewed Blackburn's license, but strongly advised him that he should seek assistance in rectifying the significant shortcomings of his establishment. It seems that Blackburn did not have the inclination to see out the required changes to the house he had occupied for the greater part of his life. Within months, Blackburn had decided to move on.

On 17th July 1903 John James Mercer, who had unsuccessfully applied for the licence for 'Our House' beer house on Halewood Road a few months previously, applied for a temporary licence to take over John Blackburn's beer house. In August, at the licensing sessions, the transfer was made permanent. With Blackburn no longer in charge, a name change for the house was in order. Mercer changed the name of the beer house to the Railway Inn, no doubt to reflect its proximity to Gateacre train station and Cheshire Lines.

In February 1908, at the annual licensing sessions at Woolton Court, the renewal of the license of the Railway Inn was objected to by Police Superintendent Baxendale on the grounds that the house was superfluous and structurally inadequate. The case was adjourned and the license renewed temporarily while the cases for and against the continued survival of the old beer house were prepared.

At the adjourned sessions in March 1908 the cases for and against the renewal of the licence of the Railway were heard. Sgt John Elsworth of the Woolton Police gave evidence that the Railway was leased by Joseph Jones and Co., brewers of Knotty Ash, and that occupant and licensee Mercer was employed by them as manager. The house was described as consisting of a small parlour and a tap room. The private accommodation was deemed poor, with the only domestic room, apart from the bedroom, being a kitchen. The sanitary provision, however, was described as good, as were the facilities for effective police supervision. The house did respectable working-class trade, but with the nearest licensed house being only 40 yards away, the police sergeant considered the house redundant due to its structural deficiencies and inadequate accommodation.

Lawyer Ernest W. Swift argued for the license of the Railway to be renewed. There had been no complaints or police action against the house or licensee, which Sgt Elsworth confirmed. Its business was respectable, and quantities sold were good, which proved the house was needed. These factors, said Swift, were reason enough to renew the licence. The magistrates retired for a short while to consider their decision, and when they resumed they deemed the Railway Inn redundant and referred the house to the quarter sessions for compensation. The license was renewed until the compensation hearing could take place. In August 1908 the decision of the Woolton court was ratified, and the Railway was awarded £1,008 in compensation, most of which was paid to the brewery. It closed its doors shortly afterwards and was never licensed again, though John Mercer remained tenant of the house for several years afterward.

The house still stands and is a private dwelling. The front window of the house has retained its distinctive wooden beer house surround.

(Fig.53) John James Mercer, successor to John Blackburn and the last licensee of the Railway Inn in Gateacre, pictured in 1922 in his 84th year. Photograph used with kind permission of Janis Winkworth

THE BROWN COW

(Fig.54) Top: The Brown Cow in 2017. It was originally a single beer house with a dwelling next door. Bottom Left: View of the north side of the pub showing the stone wall of the part of the premises built in about 1818. Bottom Right: The south side of the pub, showing the brick gable of the attached original cottage built around 1840. The two houses were knocked through into one larger pub in 1903/4.

The Brown Cow is a former beer house, open until 2020, which is on Halewood Road close to the Gateacre crossroads. Historically in the township of Much Woolton, the building itself was once two cottages, both built at different times in the first half of the 19th century, and originally owned and occupied by tailor Thomas Rushton.

In 1818 Rushton acquired a piece of land upon which he built a small sandstone house. Rushton eventually added stables at the rear, and between 1835 and 1840 built another house adjoining the first. Whereas the earlier house was built of sandstone, which can still be seen when viewing the side wall of the Brown Cow today, the new attached house was built of brick. Rushton used the new house as the dwelling for him and his family, while the old building was his tailor's shop. He also added a stable and a gig house[1] to the rear of the premises.

On 6th August 1845 Thomas Rushton died. As he was a widower, his two sons, Richard and Thomas Rushton, were named as the executors of his will. His instructions were that his premises and land were to be sold after his death, and the proceeds were to be shared between his children and grandchildren. The house, shop and land were duly offered for sale, and in 1847 they were acquired by George Fleetwood of the Tarbock Brewery, and whose family owned the Gateacre Brewery, as well as the Bear Inn and the Bull Inn. Needless to say, the sandstone house was opened as a beer house, while the attached brick cottage was let out as a dwelling.

By 1850, the beer house was occupied by Henry Turton, originally from Hale. Turton lived at the house with his wife Ann, his children and his mother. Also living with them was 13 year old servant Jane Marsh, who no doubt assisted with the running of the beer house.

By 1861 Turton and his family had moved on, with the new occupant and licensee of the beer house being Thomas Leech, originally from Frodsham, Cheshire. Leech was also a cow keeper and milk seller, and it is possibly because of this that the beer house gained its name of the Brown Cow. Leech was licensee of the Brown Cow until 1869, after which he and his wife Elizabeth moved into the attached cottage next door, leaving 30-year-old gardener George Almond from Wavertree to take over the license for the beer house. During the 1870s, when the numbering of the houses in the area became standardised, the Brown Cow became number 9 Halewood Road, with the attached cottage number 11, though this was to change again in the future.

George Almond ran the Brown Cow until his death in 1875, and his widow Elizabeth Almond took over the licence. In December that year the Beer house and attached cottage were put up for sale at an auction held at the nearby Black Bull Inn. The Premises were purchased by Andrew Barclay Walker, whose father Peter Walker had founded Walker's Brewery in Warrington. Walker also bought the Black Bull, and the Gateacre Brewery in the same auction. All indications are that Walker acquired the Brown Cow as his own personal investment, rather than on behalf of his father's brewery. Elizabeth Almond remained as licensee until February 1881, when she moved to keep a lodging house at York Cottages on nearby Grange Lane. Taking over from Almond as licensee was Walter Jones, a plumber by trade, from Poynton in Cheshire.

In February 1883 an issue was raised regarding the rear yard of the Brown Cow. It came to the attention of the Little Woolton Local Board that John Taylor, a butcher who lived on Halewood Road, was dumping the offal from his slaughter house in the pub's yard, which was not only unsavoury, but was also something of a health hazard. The Local Board wrote a letter to the Much Woolton Medical Officer to complain about the matter and to ask that it be dealt with. It seems that the matter was resolved as the issue was not raised again.

Although he ran the Brown Cow for over 10 years, not a great deal is reported about Walter Jones' time at the house, suggesting it had been fairly stable if unremarkable period. His replacement in April 1891 was James McLaughlin from Castlebar in Ireland. Upon the death of Andrew Barclay Walker in 1893, the Brown Cow was inherited by His son William Hall Walker.

At the annual licensing sessions on 25th August 1899, held at Woolton Court on Quarry Street, the licence renewal for the Brown Cow was objected to by the police. The objection stemmed from the fact that the beer house was too open at the rear, and that there were two cottages sharing a common space with the beer house. The police did not like this arrangement, as it allowed access to the house which could not be supervised and may have encouraged illicit 'back door' trading. Licensee McLaughlin also ran a coach business, for which he rented the rear yard of the Bear Inn on Gateacre Brow. This caused the police problems in determining whether persons were entering the premises of the Bear to access the inn or the coach business. The court wanted the whole situation rectifying before they would issue any licence renewals, and the hearing was adjourned. On 29th September the adjourned hearing took place, and the legal representatives of owner William Hall Walker stated that the two cottages at the rear of the Brown Cow were to be converted into stables which the licensee would use for his coach business. This also alleviated a problem faced by the Bear Inn, and on this basis, the licence was renewed. On 1st June 1900, plans drawn up by architects E.J. Slater of Liverpool, detailing the alterations that had been promised, were submitted to the court and approved.

On 23rd September 1900, a sad and tragic event occurred at the Brown Cow which shocked the inhabitants of the small village of Gateacre. It was a Sunday morning, and licensee John McLaughlin had arranged to take a day trip to Llandudno. Just before 10am his wife Elizabeth, known as 'Lizzy', saw him off and wished him a good day. At 11.20, Lizzy made her way upstairs, telling her son, Charles, who was 13 years old, that she was in pain due to a long standing complaint with her leg, and she was going to rest for a while. A short time later, young Charles went up to his mother's bedroom and found her lying on the bed. Her lips were swollen and there was a strong smell of carbolic acid. The acid bottle and a small pot were on the table at the side of the bed. Charles asked his mother what was the matter and if she had touched the bottle. She made no answer. He then asked her if he should go for a doctor, but she shook her head. Then she beckoned him to her, put her arms about his neck and told him to always be a good boy. He asked her if he could go for his aunt, and she told him he could. Charles' aunt and Lizzy's sister in law was Mary Ann Morphet, who was the wife of the licensee of 'Our House' beer house further along Halewood Road. Young Charles ran off to the house to alert her that something was wrong. In the meantime, Mary Burns, barmaid of the Brown Cow, heard a noise from upstairs, and thought that Lizzy McLaughlin had fallen out of bed. Running up, she found her lying on the floor of the room, doubled up in agony and making a gurgling sound in her throat. A short time later young Charles and Mary Ann Morphet arrived on the scene and a doctor was sent for. Attempts were made to get Lizzy to drink some water, but they were unsuccessful. At 12.15 pm, Dr Pethick arrived but stated that Lizzy was beyond all aid. She died five minutes later. A telephone call was made to Llandudno, and a message reached John McLaughlin, who returned home as fast as he was able.

On Wednesday 26th September a coroner's inquest was held at the Black Bull. John McLaughlin stated that his wife had seemed in good spirits when they had parted on Sunday morning. He told the court that she had, for some years, suffered from acute pain in her leg, which had caused her much depression. In moments of great pain she had sometimes said that she wished she was 'out of the way'. The court then heard the accounts of the witnesses who had been present on the day of Lizzy's death. The jury, having heard all the evidence, retired to consider their verdict. While they were doing so, the local church minister paid the court a visit, wanting to know what the verdict was. There was, of course, a reason for this. It just so happened that Lizzy McLoughlin's funeral was about to take place on the same day, and the minister was waiting for the verdict and the burial order. In this period a person who was found to have committed suicide would not be afforded a full Christian burial. The coroner guessed the minister's motives and so told him that the verdict was not yet decided, and sent him away. Although the jury was yet to return their verdict, the coroner issued the burial order forthwith, gave it to a person present and instructed them to make haste to with it to the minister, ensuring that Lizzy Mcloughlin was buried in a proper Christian manner. When the court reconvened, the coroner told the jury what had occurred. The jury, many of whom actually knew Lizzy, expressed indignation at the minister's actions. They returned the verdict that Lizzy had died from the effects of carbolic acid taken in a moment of temporary insanity. The coroner declared there and then that at future inquests, where the clergy similarly concerned themselves with the outcome, he would simply open the inquest, issue the burial order, and then adjourn proceedings so that the interment could take place in the meantime.

In February 1903, at the annual Childwall licensing sessions held at Woolton Court, the Brown Cow's license came up for renewal. At the time, the local magistrates were visiting all the licensed houses in the district to personally inspect them before renewing their licences. The hearing was adjourned until 13th March to allow the inspection to take place. At the adjourned hearing the bench required several improvements to the beer house. The house had several rooms, which were seen as small and cramped. There was a small bar, parlour, snug and clubroom. Access to the toilet provision in the rear yard was via the private kitchen which was also being used for drinking purposes. The court directed that a passage be constructed allowing proper access to the urinals that was not through the kitchen, and it also stipulated that the use of the kitchen for drinking had to stop. The premises was open at the back, and this was required to be rectified by the provision of a properly enclosed yard, separate from licensee McLaughlin's carriage business. The whole house was considered to be in poor condition generally. A representative of Colonel Hall Walker was present in court to receive the court's instruction, and the licence was renewed pending the drawing up of plans.

On 5th June 1903, plans were submitted by architects Medcalf and Medcalf, which they hoped would rectify the issues with the Brown Cow to the satisfaction of the court. The beer house, which was number 9 Halewood Road, was to be knocked through into number 11 next door, increasing the bedroom provision and allowing the public rooms of the house to be enlarged. A clearly defined and enclosed rear yard would be created which would cut off the beer house from the coach business, access to which would be via a passage at the side of the premises. An extension would be constructed to the front and side of the house, and a passage would be created allowing access to new toilet provision which would be separate from the kitchen. The kitchen would no longer be used for drinking purposes, but would be private. Overall the drinking space of the Brown Cow would be increased from 78 square yards to 108, and the general appearance of the beer house would be greatly improved. The police made no objections to the plans and they were approved by the court.

The alterations to the Brown Cow commenced later that year, and continued into early 1904. At the licensing sessions of the 4th February, the court were told that the extensive alterations were still being made, and that they would improve the house greatly. When the work was complete, the Brown Cow beer house had been knocked through and enlarged, and had been given a mock Tudor façade and red brick frontage, giving it the appearance it still very much retains to this day.

On 23rd March 1906 the 'bona-fide traveller question' raised its head in relation to John McLaughlin and the Brown Cow. McLaughlin was summonsed before Woolton magistrates at Quarry Street charged with having supplied two men, John Harrison and Thomas Cordling, with a pint of beer each on Sunday 4th March at 11.10 am, a time when the beer house was required to be closed. McLaughlin pleaded not guilty, citing the bona-fide traveller clause as his defence.

Superintendent Baxendale of the police outlined the case for the prosecution. He said that at the time and date in question constables Murtagh and Williams had been on duty in plain clothes for the purpose of testing bona-fide travellers. They were approaching the Brown Cow and saw licensee McLaughlin, so asked him if he had any customers in. McLaughlin replied that he had, and took the officers into the newsroom of the pub where two men were drinking beer. Constable Murtagh recognised the two men, and knew that they were from Huyton Quarry, not three miles away. The officer asked McLaughlin did he know where the men were from and the licensee replied, "Yes, from Huyton Quarry by the Seel Arms. It is over three miles away." McLaughlin stated that he knew this to be the case because, running a carriage business, he always charged 3 shillings cab fare to the Seel Arms due to the distance. The constable asked the men what the purpose of their journey was, and they replied they were going to Woolton Convalescent home to see a friend. Subsequently, the distances to the homes of the men were measured. Harrison's house was found to be 2 miles 1184 yards away, 576 yards short of 3 miles, while Cordling lived 2 miles 1727 yards away, 33 yards short of 3 miles. The prosecution's case rested on the fact that neither of the men had travelled 3 miles or more from the place where they had slept the previous night to the hostelry where they had demanded to be served and so contravened the law on bona-fide travellers.

Mr Edwin Berry, a Lawyer from Liverpool, was representing the defendants. He stated that he did not dispute the facts, but his defence of McLaughlin relied upon whether the licensee truly believed that the men were bona-fide travellers or not. If he did, argued Berry, then the magistrates should find in McLaughlin's favour. Berry then called Ina McLaughlin, the licensee's daughter, as a witness for the defence. Ina told the court that she did the books for her father's business, and knew that they charged 3 shillings from the Seel Arms based upon 1 shilling per mile. Having established where the men were from, and that they were on legitimate business to Woolton, she had no hesitation in serving them.

The magistrates decided that while a technical offence had been committed, McLaughlin and the two men would be given the benefit of the doubt. The cases against them were dismissed, provided they pay court costs. Mr Berry told the court that Sunday serving had been a source of considerable trouble to McLaughlin, and following this case he had decided to discontinue it altogether.

On New Year's Eve 1906, widower John McLaughlin married Elizabeth Lilian Hayhurst, and they had one child together. Their marriage did not prove to be harmonious and during the following year, Elizabeth left her husband on six occasions due to what she described as cruel behaviour towards her. On each occasion he had begged her to return promising to change his ways, but it appears never had. In December 1907 Elizabeth finally left McLaughlin for good, taking their child and returning to live with her mother in Wavertree. On 3rd January 1908 a case was heard at the Woolton Court to decide on maintenance for Elizabeth and the baby. John McLaughlin was described as a publican, car proprietor and rented two acres of land which was under cultivation and produced oats. He had 11 horses and 10 carriages at his stables in Gateacre, and also owned a further 2 horses and carriages which he kept at Garston. He also employed a total of six men. McLaughlin stated that the Brown Cow, which he rented from Colonel Walker, was currently running at a loss of £30 per year. As well as the child to Elizabeth, McLaughlin had six other children, three of whom were still dependent upon him. In court the claims of cruelty were not contested by McLaughlin on advice from his lawyer Mr Swift. It was agreed by all parties that he and his wife should be separated. After hearing evidence from both McLaughlin and his wife, the court made an order of 20 shillings per week maintenance to be paid to keep Elizabeth and their child.

By 1911, John McLaughlin had turned his focus upon his carriage business, while the Brown Cow was left to his son Charles to run. By the end of the following year, the McLaughlins had left the pub, and a new licensee was to take over. In December 1912, a temporary transfer of the license for the Brown Cow was granted to John Farrelly, who had 20 years' experience in the licensing trade in Liverpool. Farrelly took up occupancy, paying a rent of £30 per annum to Colonel Hall Walker, and at the licensing sessions on 6th February 1913 the transfer was made permanent.

In October 1917, the Brown Cow beer house was offered up for sale at a property auction held at the nearby Black Bull. Colonel Walker was moving from Gateacre to a new residence in Denbighshire, and as a consequence his former assets in and around the area were being sold. The Brown Cow was acquired by the Crown Brewery based in Birkdale. John Farrelly remained as licensee until June 1924, when transfer was granted to Mrs Amy Edwards. In January 1931 the licence was acquired by Mary Jane Rothwell, and in 1937 the licensee was Catherine Agnes Christian, who ran the pub throughout the Second World War.

Eventually, as with all the surviving old beer houses, the Brown Cow became a fully licensed house, the last vestiges of the Beer House Act having long since become defunct. The former beer house survived as one of Gateacre Village's three remaining public houses until March 2020 when the Coronavirus pandemic struck, and pubs across the country were forced to close their doors. When the national lockdown eased later that year the nearby Black Bull and Bear Staff were able to reopen, subject to certain conditions. The smaller Brown Cow, however, did not reopen, and, as this book heads towards publication, remains closed. Looking increasingly neglected, there are fears the historic former beer house could become a permanent victim of the pandemic. There is still a hope that with a new tenant, and perhaps a little investment, the Brown Cow may welcome customers through its doors again at some point in the future.

Notes:

[1]A gig was a light, two wheeled carriage pulled by a single horse.

THE FOLLY VALE TAVERN

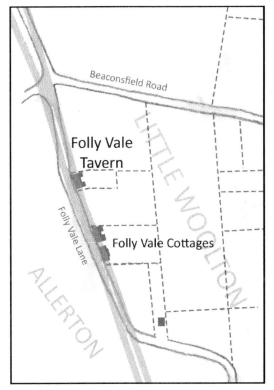

(Fig.55) Map showing the location of George Houghton's Folly Vale tavern in the mid-19th century. This section of Folly Vale Lane is now Menlove Avenue. Both the tavern and Folly Vale Cottages were demolished to make way for the mansion house of Robert Gladstone in 1869. The modern dual carriageway is overlaid, showing how the south bound carriageway runs through the spot where the Folly Vale Tavern once stood.

The Folly Vale Tavern was a beer house that stood within Little Woolton on what was once part of Vale Road but is now Menlove Avenue. The old house is long gone, as is the grand house which replaced it.

In the 17th century an area of land bordering with the township of Allerton, near to what is now the junction of Vale Road and Menlove Avenue, was referred to as Hunt's Folly. By the 19th century it had become known as Folly Vale, and prior to 1870 Vale Road was called Folly Vale Lane. The old road continued on past the end of Beaconsfield Road, following the course of the modern dual carriageway which was built over it in the early 20th Century. In Folly Vale was a clutch of old, small cottages known as Folly Vale Cottages, and a little further on from them nearer to the junction with Beaconsfield Road, was another cottage and garden.

Around 1840 the cottage and garden was occupied by George and Ann Houghton and their family. Houghton, a wheelwright by trade, and originally from Halewood, opened his cottage as a beer house which became known as the Folly Vale Tavern. In 1857, Houghton's wife Ann died aged only 47 years of age after what was described as a long and painful illness.

In 1868, the land upon which George Houghton's house and the nearby Folly Vale Cottages stood was sold to Robert Gladstone. After nearly three decades running his beer house, Houghton had to relinquish his occupancy and move on. He held the beer license at the Old House at Home beer house in Ashton Square, Woolton for a short time. But by 1870 he was living on Quarry Street where he was plying his trade as a wheelwright. In 1873 Houghton was again a licensee, running the Halfway House beer house on Belle Vale Road, Gateacre.

By 1869 the Folly Vale Cottages and the old beer house had been demolished and Gladstone built a grand house called Woolton Vale on the site. The entrance to the driveway of the house was approximately where the Folly Vale Tavern had stood.

Woolton Vale, which later became a children's home, has itself since been demolished. The site of the Folly Vale Tavern is now occupied by the dual carriageway that is Menlove Avenue.

GATEACRE BREWERY

(Fig.56) The former Gateacre Brewery on Gateacre Brow, built in 1830[1] by John Fleetwood. To the right of the picture is the 'commodious dwelling house' Fleetwood built for himself and his family to live in, and where successive proprietors of the brewery lived.

The Gateacre Brewery has been a prominent feature of the village for nearly two centuries. The brewery was built by John Fleetwood, born in Eccleston, the son of a brewer, also called John Fleetwood.

John Fleetwood senior was born in 1765 in Cheshire and was the son of a farmer. His early years were spent as a husbandman, but he entered the brewing trade, moving to Eccleston where he and his wife Mary had a four sons and two daughters. Three of their sons, John junior born in 1799, William born in 1801 and George born in 1806, were to enter either the brewing or licensing trade. Eldest son, Thomas, did not enter the brewing trade, and instead became a cooper.

In the early 19th century John Fleetwood senior became proprietor of his own brewery, leasing the Tarbock Brewery from the Earl of Derby. He lived at an estate in Ditton, and employed his son George to run his brewery. He also acquired a public house in Key Street, Liverpool called the Wheatsheaf, and a number of cottages nearby.

In May 1830, John Fleetwood senior died. In his will he left his public house, and his brewery in Tarbock to son George. He also ensured that his wife and other children were well taken care of financially.

Later that year, John Fleetwood junior, who had purchased a piece of land on Gateacre Brow in 1829, built the brewery which became known as the Gateacre Brewery. The building of the brewery was very timely, as the new 1830 Beerhouse Act was to create a sharp increase in demand for beer to supply the numerous beer houses which were to spring up in the vicinity over the next few years. In 1834 John's brother, William also entered the licensing trade and became the owner of the Bear Inn on Gateacre Brow, purchasing it from the executors of late owner Richard Webster.

John Fleetwood's new brewery was built 'on the most approved principle, regardless of expense'. The premises included a commodious dwelling house where John lived with his family. The building of the brewery, and the purchase of the Bear Inn, was the beginning of the dominance of the Fleetwood family in terms of brewing and licensing in Gateacre Village which would last for nearly half a century. However, the Fleetwood family's tenure in charge of Gateacre's brewery and public houses was not an altogether fortuitous one, in fact it could very well be said to have been cursed.

In 1836, misfortune struck the family for the first time since moving to Gateacre. John Fleetwood, after only six years as owner of his own brewery, died at the young age of 37 years. The executors of John's will included his brother George, of the Tarbock Brewery, James Longton of Much Woolton and Thomas Cross, who was described as a gentleman of Little Woolton. John Fleetwood's instructions regarding the brewery were quite precise. The business was to be kept as a going concern, with Thomas Cross to act as proprietor. This was until either John Fleetwood's youngest son, 9 year old John, had reached the age of 24 years, whereupon the brewery and estate was to be sold, or until any of his sons – again having reached the age of 24 – raised the capital to purchase the brewery themselves in the meantime. The other sons of the late John Fleetwood were eldest Henry, who was 12 at the time of his father's death, and James, who was 10 years old. Thomas Cross, and his wife Ellen, were also appointed guardians of John Fleetwood's children, and moved to live with them at the brewery house.

As if John Fleetwood's death at only 37 years old wasn't tragic enough for the family, John's brother, William, was to die less than a year later. William Fleetwood was the owner of the Bear Inn which was situated just a little further up Gateacre Brow, and in 1837 he died of consumption aged only 36 years. The inn was inherited by his wife Hannah.

The Fleetwood family further strengthened their grip on the licensing trade in Gateacre when, in about 1845, the Bull Inn was acquired by Henry Fleetwood, eldest son of the late Gateacre Brewery builder John Fleetwood. Then, in 1847, George Fleetwood of the Tarbock brewery bought a house on Halewood Lane (now Halewood *Road*) at auction, which he turned into the beer house which became the Brown Cow. The family now owned the brewery and three licensed houses in the immediate vicinity.

Thomas Cross ran the Gateacre Brewery as a trustee until his death in 1845. The business was maintained as going concern until, in 1848, James Fleetwood attained the age of 24 years and purchased the brewery, house and land under the name of James Fleetwood and Co. However, within only two years of James becoming owner of the brewery, the three Fleetwood brothers died in quick succession. In November 1850, John Fleetwood junior died aged only 23 years, and in December 1850, brewery owner James Fleetwood died aged 25 years, after suffering an epileptic fit. Less than a year later, eldest brother Henry, owner of the Bull Inn, died aged 27. The brothers died intestate, and with no eligible heirs. The brewery and the Bull Inn were put up for sale at an auction which was to be held in the Bull Inn in January 1852.

When it was advertised for sale in the months preceding the auction, the Gateacre Brewery was described as a 'substantial' brewery sitting on 3100 square yards of land, with offices, stables, shippons and other outbuildings, as well as a large dwelling house and garden for the occupation of the owner or manager. Also owned by the brewery were the two houses adjoining the brewery on Gateacre Brow which were let as dwellings[2].

The chance of the brewery and licensed houses being bought by someone outside of the Fleetwood family was averted. George Fleetwood, who for two decades had owned the Tarbock Brewery, stepped in and bought the Gateacre Brewery and the Bull Inn. Fleetwood then gave control of the Gateacre Brewery to his son, George Fleetwood junior, who was only 20. Young George Fleetwood moved to Gateacre with his wife Anne and took up residency in the brewery house, while George Fleetwood senior's trusted and respected brewery clerk John Gregory was installed as manager under young George. Gregory had gained valuable experience of the brewing trade at the Tarbock brewery, and George Fleetwood senior had known him since he had been a young boy. In the light of his son's youth and inexperience, George senior turned to Gregory to conduct the 'hands on' running of the business in Gateacre.

In 1855 widow Hannah Fleetwood died, and the Bear Inn was also purchased by George Fleetwood senior. Brewery manager John Gregory, took occupancy of the Bear and became its licensee for several years, until in 1864 he relinquished the licence to focus on his duties at the brewery. John Gregory and his brother Thomas were becoming more involved in the brewing and licensing trade. In the 1860s and 1870s, Thomas Gregory was master brewer at the Aigburth Brewery, which he rented from the Trustees of Thomas Bailey, and the brothers also began to add ownership of several public houses to their portfolio, such as the Oddfellows Arms in Woolton. The empire of the Gregory brothers would continue to grow, and it wouldn't be too long before it exceeded even that of their mentors the Fleetwood family.

In 1867, misfortune again struck the Fleetwood family, when George Fleetwood junior died aged only 35 years old. His wife Anne continued to oversee the Gateacre Brewery, and some years later would even add the Cobden Vaults beer house in Quarry Street, Woolton, to her portfolio.

In 1869, brewery manager John Gregory, a widower after the death of his wife Sarah in 1863, married Elizabeth Taylor, the daughter of beer house licensee William Taylor of the Dukes Vaults in Woolton. Gregory moved into the beer house on 37 Allerton Road and became its licensee.

It appears that splitting his time between running the Dukes Vaults and managing the Gateacre Brewery was proving impractical for Gregory. In 1871 he decided to retire from his position at the brewery in order to focus on his own business interests. On the 2nd February a lavish farewell supper and ball was laid on by Anne Fleetwood. 150 guests were treated to a banquet in a large room at the brewery which had been decorated for the occasion. Head of the proceedings was patriarch George Fleetwood, who had recently retired to Shropshire leaving the Tarbock Brewery in the control of his son Edward. Speeches were made in Gregory's honour, and another of the brewery's rooms had been laid out as a ballroom where the guests danced to a quadrille band until the early hours. And so John Gregory moved on from the brewery, and his position as manager was taken by a Mr Hazelwoode, who was promoted into the position. However, in what was probably unforeseen at the time, it would not be too long before Gregory would be back at the brewery, though in a different capacity.

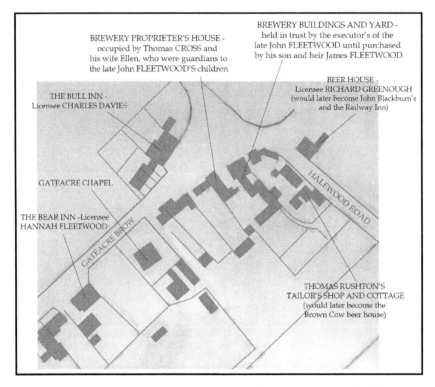

(Fig. 57) A map of Gateacre in 1840, based on a survey conducted that year and published in 1843.

In 1872, Anne Fleetwood was remarried to Robert Cargill, and by 1873 she had moved away, leaving the running and management of the brewery in the hands of a group of trustees led by the brewery manager. With Anne and her new husband planning to emigrate to Canada, the brewery house stood empty, though the brewery itself was operated by the trustees for the next few years. By the time Anne Cargill left Gateacre, she had left behind an era in which a succession of Fleetwood brewers and licensees had all died before the age of forty.

In 1875 old George Fleetwood put the brewery, the Bull Inn and Brown Cow up for sale. In stepped Andrew Barclay Walker, himself a wealthy brewer and local Gateacre resident. Walker bought the brewery, along with the Bull Inn and Brown Cow, as well as the Cobden Vaults in Woolton. Ownership of the Bear Inn, however, was passed from George Fleetwood to his son Edward, who had succeeded his father as proprietor of the Tarbock Brewery. No doubt it made sense for the Fleetwoods to retain at least one outlet for their ale in Gateacre.

The change in ownership of the brewery heralded a return to Gateacre for John Gregory. John and his brother Thomas rented the Gateacre Brewery from Walker, with John and his family taking occupancy of the Gateacre Brewery house. Thomas relinquished his position at the Aigburth Brewery and moved to Gateacre to be more involved with the new business. The one time employees of the Fleetwoods were now the proprietors of their former brewery.

Andrew Barclay Walker was owner of the brewery until 1878, when the Gregory brothers bought it from him outright. The Gregorys enjoyed more fortune whilst in charge of the Gateacre Brewery than did their predecessors the Fleetwoods, and became arguably even more dominant in the area. They went on to acquire numerous public houses in the district, including several in Woolton and Garston. In 1886 they bought the Aigburth Brewery, where Thomas had once been master brewer, and acquired the Tarbock Brewery upon the retirement from the business of Edward Fleetwood. The two men who, many years before, had worked at the brewery under George Fleetwood, one as a humble clerk and one as a gardener, were now the owners of a considerable local brewing empire. John Gregory resided at the Gateacre Brewery, while his brother Thomas lived at the Brewery House in Tarbock.

In February 1892 John Gregory died aged 69 years, leaving his brother Thomas as sole owner of their breweries and public houses. Thomas' son Charles Gregory moved in to take charge of the Gateacre Brewery until his death in 1903, at only 41 years old. Upon Charles' death, Thomas Gregory's only remaining son, William Henry, took over at the Gateacre Brewery

Thomas Gregory died in February 1909 in his 84th year, and was buried at the parish church in Halewood. The brewery fell into the hands of his executors, and remained so for many years afterwards, though it continued to be managed by Thomas' son, William.

By 1921 the brewery had ceased operations and was divided into two dwellings numbered 42 and 42A Gateacre Brow. Over the next 11 years it was inhabited by various occupants, until in 1932 Arthur Clegg & Son acquired the old brewery and turned it into a 'flock' or felt factory. Clegg had for many years been a marine store dealer, and had a premises in Almond Street, Liverpool and were branching out into felt manufacturing.

Clegg's Felt Factory remained in business for over 70 years, eventually ceasing operations in 2003. The former brewery and factory has since been converted into dwellings, and further development has taken place on the site with the construction of modern apartment blocks in the former factory's grounds.

(Fig. 58) Another view of the Gateacre Brewery dwelling house built by John Fleetwood in 1830, and home to a succession of the brewery's proprietors over the years that followed.

Notes:

[1]Although built in 1830, local architectural historians Janet Gnospellius and John Dewsnap suggest that the Brewery may have been rebuilt, or at least renovated, in the 1850s or 1860s. Although there appears to be no documentary evidence for this, the building has certain features which they argue are consistent with other buildings of this period, i.e. 'brick, stone cornice and bands, surface decorated with lozenges and circles of blue and yellow brick - polychromatic fashion c.f. All Saints, Margaret St., Architect Wm. Butterfield c.1850' (Gateacre Society Walk Notes, 16 July 1977). While this architectural assessment carries weight, it remains to be seen why the relatively new brewery would be rebuilt and who would go to such expense.

[2]These houses would become number 38 and 40 Gateacre Brow when the numbering system was introduced in the 1870s.

THE GATEACRE SHOOTING INCIDENT

In 1895 a shooting incident took place on Belle Vale Road in Gateacre which was something of a local sensation at the time, and which provides an insight into the social attitudes of the period. The case, which ended up in Liverpool Assizes, revolved around the old aphorism that 'a man's home is his castle'[1] and the principle that he is allowed to defend it by any reasonable means.

The incident itself took place on 23rd September 1895 and involved Gateacre farmer, dairyman and cart owner James Guy. Guy was accused of having shot a labourer called James Gallagher, from Rose Street, Woolton, with intent to cause him grievous bodily harm. Standing as witnesses for Gallagher were his brother, Patrick Gallagher, and another male called Patrick Coll. The case initially appeared before the Woolton Magistrates court on 25th October, where Police Superintendent Baxendale made out the case for the prosecution. It was the duty of the magistrates to consider whether there was enough evidence for the case to be sent to the Liverpool Assizes to be tried by judge and jury.

The defendant James Guy lived on Belle Vale Road, near to Gateacre Railway Station. At the time of the incident, work was taking place on the installation of a new sewer in that road, and Guy was employed there with his cart, transporting materials to and from the site. The sewer, the first to be laid in Little Woolton[2], required a degree of casual labour which was arranged on a day to day basis by foreman or 'ganger' Thomas Wise.

Superintendent Baxendale told the court that the two Gallaghers and Coll, along with about eleven other men, had gone to the site of the sewer works to look for employment for the day. The three men had been in the Brown Cow beer house and had a couple of pints of beer each before approaching foreman Wise and asking him if there was any work to be had. Wise had told them there was no work for them, but when they saw Guy working nearby one of the men said, "There's the one who is preventing us getting work." The prosecution then alleged that Guy threw stones at the three men, whereupon they chased Guy to his house which was not far away. It is alleged Guy went into his house, emerging moments later with a double barrelled shotgun. Guy is said to have pointed the gun at the men and, with no warning discharged it, shooting James Gallagher in the shoulder. Gallagher was taken to Brownlow Hill Workhouse Hospital in Liverpool where he was treated, and was still suffering from the injuries he had received. This was the prosecution case in summary, and Superintendent Baxendale argued that it should be enough for the matter to be put before a jury.

Barrister Mr Segar was defending Guy, and he set about cross examining the three Woolton men. It was then that the case began to unravel somewhat. Mr Segar put a number of points to the men which he based upon Guy's account of the incident. Mr Segar asked them was it not the case that after being turned down for work by Wise, they saw Guy working and let fly a number of expletives, saying "He's the one we want" and "Mates, go for him," after which they attacked him with stones causing him to flee. The men denied this, and also denied that Coll had grabbed hold of Guy, ripping his shirt, and that after Guy had entered his house, they had stood outside shouting "Bring him out here and we will kill him," and "we will have his life." It was alleged by Mr Segar that the language used by the three men was peppered with cursing of the worst sort.

Segar accused James Gallagher of having borne a grudge against Guy since 1890, after an incident in Gateacre where Gallagher had been drunk and was attacking a policeman. During the occurrence, Guy had gone to the officer's aid and had assisted him in subduing Gallagher. Since that time Gallagher had regularly threatened Guy when he had been in Belle Vale Road. In 1892, claimed Segar, Gallagher entered a field where Guy was working and threatened to run him through with a pitchfork. It was also brought up in court that Gallagher had been discharged from the army for fighting, had several convictions for assaulting the police, as well as numerous others for violence and for being drunk and disorderly. It was further alleged that Gallagher was well known for demanding money with menaces, approaching workmen at sites demanding money for drink, and entering public houses and threatening staff and customers if they did not provide him with liquor. Mr Segar claimed that on the very day of the incident the men had only had the money to buy beer in the Brown Cow because Gallagher had threatened a man called Riley into giving him a shilling. Gallagher denied having a grudge against Guy, and demanding money with menaces, stating that the male called Riley had given him a shilling of his own free will.

Other witnesses were then called who backed up Guy's story. Foreman Wise stated that he had heard the men threaten Guy, as well as witnessing them throw stones at him. He had not seen Guy throw any stones in return. Another witness, a sewerage engineer called Green, testified that he saw the three men attacking Guy with stones, and also attacking his house with stones causing damage to the door. Guy, he stated, had done nothing to provoke this.

When James Guy was questioned he gave his version of events. He talked of being attacked with stones, having his house damaged and being threatened with his life. The stones had been thrown towards his head, and damage to his door at head height proved it. Having fled into his house with the three men still threatening him outside, he had gone to his door with the gun and warned the men to stop or he would be forced to use it. Still fearing for his life, he had fired the gun, which was loaded with bird shot, at James Gallagher.

In evidence, Police Inspector Pickering described how, when he attended the scene, he found James Gallagher lying in the road injured and subsequently took Guy into custody. Guy admitted to the Inspector that he had shot Gallagher, stating he thought it lawful to do so to defend himself and his property. Inspector Pickering admitted to the court that Guy had always been a man of good character and the Gallaghers and Coll were well known to the police.

The defending Barrister then made a plea to the court. He moved that the case go no further and that it would be a waste of time and money to initiate proceedings at the higher court. He argued that Guy was entitled in law to defend his life by firing that gun, and that Gallagher was in the very act of throwing a stone at Guy's head when he was shot. He only did what was necessary to defend himself and his property. It was, Mr Segar argued, an unpleasant thing to see a man of Guy's character, who had been 15 years at the farm and was much respected and well known, to be placed in the dock due to the spurious accusations of three ruffians. "If these three foul mouthed ruffians and dangerous characters," said Segar, "who armed themselves with dangerous weapons, got a little sparrow shot to stir them up no one could be blamed but themselves." It was put to the bench that no jury would convict under such circumstances. Having retired to consider Mr Segar's plea, the bench returned and decided to commit the case to the assizes for trial.

The Gateacre shooting case was put before Mr Justice Collins at the Liverpool Assizes on 22nd November. The evidence was put before the court in much the same way as it had at the Woolton Magistrates Court. It was not far into the hearing when the judge called a halt to proceedings. He had decided that even at this early stage, the evidence pointed to the fact that James Guy was merely taking reasonable means to protect himself from a formidable attack by three ruffians. The case was discontinued and Guy was told he was free to go. He was greeted in the corridor by numerous cheering and clapping Gateacre residents.

Notes:

[1]This is the phrase used by lawyer Mr Segar in his defence of James Guy, though the more familiar phrase is 'an Englishman's home is his castle'.

[2]There had been a sewer laid beneath Gateacre Brow a number of years previously, but that belonged to the township of Much Woolton. Several of the better off Little Woolton residents living nearby paid the Much Woolton Local Board a fee to have their drains connected to it.

THE PERIL OF THE DEADLY 'RED HILL'

(Fig.59) Top Left: The deceptive crest of Woolton Hill Road which hides the steep decline beyond. Top Right: The long slope down which Victorian cyclists built up a dangerous rate of velocity. Bottom left: The unforgiving wall of the Grange against which several cyclists met their death. Bottom Right: The view up Woolton Hill Road from the Grange. The junction was widened considerably in the mid-20th century. Though it looks far less imposing now, it was the scourge of Victorian and Edwardian vehicles with their rudimentary and inefficient braking systems.

Woolton Hill Road runs from Rose Brow, opposite Gateacre Grange, up the hill and towards Allerton. It was constructed following the Enclosures Act of 1805 as a preserved route across the former commons and to provide access to the house and estate of Thomas Rawson who lived at Rose Hill. Being on Woolton Hill the road is naturally steep, and this has caused numerous problems for horse drawn vehicles and bicycles in centuries past. In one period, in the late 19th and early 20th centuries, Woolton Hill Road gained a degree of notoriety which earned it the local nickname of the 'Red Hill', so frequent and often serious were the accidents that occurred there. This period of infamy was in great part due to the rise in popularity of bicycles as a means of personal transport and leisure in the late Victorian era.

The road was not so perilous for those ascending the hill, as it was for those travelling in the opposite direction. Cart or coach drivers could negotiate the steep decline by applying the brake to the rear wheel and then allowing the horse or horses to drag the vehicle down the decline, disengaging the brake when the vehicle was on the level again. This must have been common practice at the time, so much so that the Much and Little Woolton Urban Councils had a local byelaw to protect the road surfaces. On 30th September 1898 Constable Rutter of the Woolton Police was on duty when he witnessed a carter from Liverpool called George Lumb driving down Woolton Hill Road in his vehicle. Lumb had locked the rear wheel of his cart for the descent but was not using a skid pan. The local byelaw required the use of a skid pan under a locked wheel to prevent damage to the road. The constable reported Lumb who appeared at the Quarry Street court in October. He told the magistrates he did not know about the offence, as he was from Liverpool where there was no such law in force. He was fined 1 shilling and 4 shillings costs.

The situation was different for cyclists, especially those unfamiliar with the area. Having crested the relatively level summit, they would find themselves in a severe and unexpected decline. In the days of bicycles having rudimentary brakes, if they had any at all, this caused deadly chaos. What served as the *coup de grace* was the eight foot high stone wall of Gateacre Grange that awaited the unwary road user at the foot of the hill. There are a number of examples from the Victorian and Edwardian eras of the treacherous nature of Woolton Hill Road.

In the late 1800s, the Red Hill had already garnered something of a reputation amongst the local inhabitants of Gateacre and Woolton. However, visitors who were unfamiliar with the area often unwittingly found themselves at its mercy, with tragic consequences. On Saturday 10th April 1897, it claimed a victim in an accident involving 24 year old cyclist Selina Williams from Toxteth. At about 3.30pm Selina, along with three others – Thomas Williams, Robert Williams and Maud Goodman – were out cycling when they reached the crest of Woolton Hill Road. Thomas Williams had no brake on his bike, so he and two of the others with him dismounted, in order to push their bicycles down the hill. Selina, however, carried on riding past them, entering the sharp decline of the road. Maud Goodman shouted to her to ask did she have her brake on, to which she replied she did, however it soon appeared that Selina was dangerously out of control. Unable to stop, she sped down the hill, dashed across Rose Brow, and struck the wall of the Grange with terrible force. Selina's head impacted with the wall and she was killed instantly. Selina's body was carried into the Grange, and the local medical officer, Dr Chisholm, was summoned. He pronounced her dead, and her body was removed to the nearby Black Bull Hotel to await an inquest.

The inquest was held at the Black Bull the following Monday. The jury inspected the badly damaged bicycle, and then listened to the accounts of the witnesses. Thomas Williams, the deceased's brother, stated that Selina was an experienced cyclist, but that they had not seen the signs at the top of the hill warning cyclists of the dangerous descent. Discussion then followed as to Selina's experience, which it transpired was only six months cycling, and mainly on the flat. A conversation also took place as to why the party did not see the warning sign, which had been erected in June 1896 by the Little Woolton Local Board. The members of the party on that day stated they had not seen any signs, and had they done so would have ensured that Selina dismounted with them. Inspector Adamson of the local police also gave evidence, and stated that the warning sign in question was virtually useless, being only 2 feet by 1 foot 3 inches in size, and very easy to miss. The Inspector stated that in the last four years alone there had been an accident which resulted in a man dying in hospital, another accident whereby the injured party had needed a metal plate inserting into his skull, and four other incidents after which persons had to be transported home. Evidence was heard from several witnesses who had experienced difficulties in descending the hill, some of whom had narrowly escaped serious injury or death. Suggestions were then made as to what should be done to prevent future incidents at the location, with a debate taking place as to the effectiveness of brakes on bicycles, and the fact that many bicycles did not have brakes fitted at all. The inquest explored the option of asking Colonel Hall Walker to rebuild the wall of the Grange further back from the pavement and planting bushes in front of it to break the momentum of cyclists who found themselves in trouble. This was deemed unnecessary, and it was decided that the real issue was the deceptive nature of the road and the lack of adequate warning signs. A point was made that cyclists proceeding along what initially seemed a moderate declivity, were unprepared for the sudden drop they found themselves upon. The coroner concluded that although the National Cyclists' Union had a primary responsibility to erect warning signs in places of danger, and very often did so, the Little Woolton Local Board had a professional and moral obligation to make the roads in their district safe. They were duty-bound to erect warning signs at the top of Woolton Hill Road which were of sufficiently size and visibility. In the case of Selina Williams, the jury returned a verdict of accidental death.

Only a short time after this incident, another fatality was fortuitously avoided in the same place. On the 1st May 1897, a young man whose name was not reported, found himself in difficulties descending the hill and lost control of his bicycle. He was able to throw himself off the machine just as he reached the junction, and, although he was hurt, he escaped serious injury. His bike went on to collide with the wall of the Grange and was smashed into pieces.

The tragic death of Miss Williams prompted the Reverend Charles Yeld, vicar of Grassendale, to write to the local newspaper. Published on the 5th June 1897, it read: '*Since the last fatal accident at the bottom of Woolton Hill Road and the recommendation of the coroner, I believe nothing has been done to lessen the danger to cyclists on this most perilous bit of road. I am informed that the owner of the property does not see his way to removing the stone wall which, running at right angles to the hill, proved so disastrous to riders. Will you allow me to suggest a very simple remedy, which would, I believe, obviate all risk in the future? If the road authorities would lay down three yards of loose granite pebbles at the top of the hill where the decline begins, no cyclist having any regard for his machine and his own comfort would think of riding over these. He would dismount ; and seeing a well displayed warning of the danger of the hill would either not mount again till he had walked down to the bottom or would go with great care and so avoid the present awful risk. The very slight inconvenience to cart or carriage traffic would be as nothing compared with the terrible damage which has already been done and is likely to occur any day unless effective precautions are taken.*' It appears the Reverend Yeld's suggestion did not gain the attention of the authorities, or if it did was never given any credence and acted upon.

On 12th August 1898, Woolton Hill Road claimed another victim, in the person of Richard Leigh from Market Drayton. That day, Richard and his brother George Leigh had been cycling to Woolton to meet with friends. They had intended to make their way along Church Road into Woolton Village, but being unfamiliar with the area found themselves on Woolton Hill Road, having no idea of its steep nature. It was ten past midnight and dark, and the two men did not see the warning signs. At the same time, two local police officers, Sergeant Johnson and Constable Rutter were walking along the road when they saw the two cyclists travelling at great speed. Richard Leigh had taken his feet off the pedals and had them on the foot rests. Sergeant Johnson shouted a warning to the men, and George Leigh managed to dismount. Richard Leigh, however, lost control of his machine and, unable to stop or take evasive action, slammed into the wall of the Grange. The bicycle was shattered to pieces, and Leigh sustained a fractured skull and lower jaw, as well as multiple cuts. He was taken to a cottage nearby, where the police sergeant did his best to dress the wounds. The local doctor, Dr Vereker, was called for, and he recommended Leigh be transported to Liverpool Infirmary. Leigh later died of his injuries.

Despite Woolton Hill's growing notoriety, and the recommendations made following the case of Selina Williams, the danger of the Red Hill persisted and it struck again on 17th September 1899. On this occasion the victim was 25 year old Jeremiah Beattie, a blacksmith from Liverpool. Beattie had spent the afternoon cycling in the district, and at about 7pm he found himself at the top of Woolton Hill Road. Either failing to see or disregarding the warning signs, Beattie entered the descent and had decided to coast to the bottom, taking his feet off the pedals and placing them on the foot rests. At the same time, Mr Herbert Leventon of Gateacre was walking down Woolton Hill Road when he saw Beattie riding past him, travelling at great speed. Leventon tried to shout a warning to Beattie, but it was either not heard or ignored. When he reached the bottom, at the junction with Rose Brow, he struck the kerb opposite and was catapulted into the wall of the Grange. A number of people rushed to his aid, and the unconscious man was taken to Grange Cottages nearby and medical assistance was called for. Beattie, who had a fractured skull and jaw, was taken by horse cab to the Liverpool Royal Infirmary where he died of his injuries. An inquest was held at the Liverpool Coroner's Court, and it was established that warning signs were present and visible at the top of the hill, and Beattie's bicycle had a brake. It did not appear that Beattie had applied his brake, as the witness Leventon said he would have heard it, but it was generally accepted that it would not have worked anyway given the speed at which he was descending the hill. The coroner inferred that Beattie had been reckless to ignore the warnings and to ride in such a manner. A verdict of accidental death was returned.

As well as the fatalities, there were those who had lucky escapes. On 22nd March 1902, St Helens glass maker Arthur Birkbeck received what was described as an 'object lesson' for cyclists. On the afternoon in question, Birkbeck and his friend John Jones were cycling down the Woolton Hill when Birkbeck lost control of his machine. Gathering speed and unable to stop, Birkbeck was able to throw himself from his bike moments before impact with the wall of the Grange. His head collided with the kerb stones, and he was rendered unconscious. He was taken by horse cab to the surgery of local medical officer Dr Petherick. Thankfully, Birkbeck only had concussion and regained consciousness after 30 minutes. He was transported to Huyton railway station, accompanied by Jones and local Police Constable Fairclough, where he was able to get the train home.

On 23rd November 1913, Woolton Hill claimed another life. On this occasion it was not a cyclist, but a police officer driving a patrol wagon. In the early hours of Sunday morning,

Constable Samuel Jonah Smart was driving the wagon, pulled by a single horse, and was accompanied by Constable Robert Hugh Summerville. The officers were from the Old Swan division, and were on their way to Woolton Police Station to collect a prisoner to convey to the Liverpool Magistrates Court in Dale Street. Smart was considered an experienced and careful driver. The officers were not completely familiar with the area, and upon reaching the top of Woolton Hill Road, instead of taking one of the other more direct roads to Quarry Street, took the turning onto the hill itself. At that time the gas lamps had been extinguished, and the darkness was intensified by the branches of large trees overhanging the road on both sides. As they reached the dip of the road, the horse started galloping, but on the steep decline the wagon overtook it, and the ironwork of the vehicle struck the horse's legs, the reins of the horse going slack. With Smart being unable to control the horse or the wagon, the vehicle careered towards the kerb. When the wagon hit the kerb stones and mounted the pavement, Smart was thrown from his seat and the wagon ran over him. The seat of the wagon was fixed well above the height of the horse, the driver being head and shoulders above the top of the vehicle. The only thing to stop him being thrown forward was the slanting foot board. Smart was a heavy man, and it is believed he hit the ground with some force. The wagon continued along the pavement, and began to scrape along the stone wall. This began to slow it down, and Constable Summerville was able to grab the reins and regain control of the horse, bringing the vehicle to a halt. He was able to quieten the panicked horse, and then ran back to help his colleague. He loaded him onto the wagon and took him to Woolton Police station on Quarry Street. Constable Smart was transferred by horse ambulance to Liverpool Infirmary, where he died some hours later of internal injuries. The patrol Wagon and prisoner still had to be returned to Liverpool, and Constable Summerville enlisted the help of Constable Ferguson. On the way back the horse tried to bolt, and both men struggled to control it, though eventually they were able to lead it back to Dale Street. An inquest was held, and Constable Summerville gave evidence, explaining the circumstances of the event. The jury returned a verdict of accidental death, but that both the insufficient lighting on Woolton Hill Road, and the height of the seat on the police vehicle were contributing factors. Constable Smart was only 12 months from retirement and left a wife and five children.

Accidents continued to occur on the Red Hill well into the 20th century, for example in July 1915, when a male called William Bryden from Liverpool lost control of his bicycle while descending the hill, smashing into the Grange wall and receiving serious injuries. But the dawning of the age of the motor vehicle, and advancements in braking systems for bicycles, has led to Woolton Hill Road posing far less of a risk to road users than it once did. The junction where the road meets Rose Brow and the Grange has been considerably enlarged in the mid-20th century, with Rose Brow itself now more than twice its original width. Although still quite steep, Woolton Hill is a far less daunting proposition for cyclists.

Woolton Hill has been an enduring feature of Woolton, Gateacre and the surrounding the area for many centuries, and has played a major part in defining its identity; from the days of the hill lookers of the manor court, the ancient windmills, Isaac Greene's summer house, and the enclosure of the commons. Its relatively brief spell as the Red Hill has had no less significant an impact on the lives of the past inhabitants of the area, and is a part of the history of Gateacre which is worthy of remembrance.

PRINCIPAL SOURCES
AND REFERENCES

Records of the Lancashire Estates of the Marquess of Salisbury (Liverpool Record Office)

The Norris Papers, Court Rolls of Woolton Parva, 1547-1587 (facsimile LRO)

An Act for inclosing lands in the Manors or Townships of Childwall, Great Woolton and Little Woolton, in the Parish of Childwall, in the County Palatine of Lancaster, 1797-1805 (Knowsley Hall Estate Office)

Little Woolton out-township records 1867-1913 (Liverpool Record Office)

Much Woolton out-township records 1867-1913 (Liverpool Record Office)

Records of Culshaw and Sumner, Architects and Surveyors of Liverpool, Grange Estate Little Woolton (Lancashire Archives)

Records of Culshaw and Sumner, Architects and Surveyors of Liverpool, plan of a copyhold estate in Little Woolton, surveyed for Mr Case, December 1854 (Lancashire Archives)

Archdeaconry of Chester Probate Records, 1661 – 1845 (Lancashire Archives) wills of Henry Orme (1661), John Fleetwood (1830), John Fleetwood (1836), Richard Greenough (1844), Thomas Rushton (1845)

Land Tax Assessments for the Townships of Much Woolton, Little Woolton and Childwall 1781-1831 (Lancashire Archives)

Alehouse Recognizances for the West Derby Hundred, Prescot Division 1753-1828 (Lancashire Archives)

UK Census Records 1841-1911

Plan of the Allotments in Childwall 1813

Plan of the Allotments of Little Woolton Common 1813

Yates and Perry Map of Liverpool and its environs 1768

Lancashire Tithe Apportionments for Much Woolton, Little Woolton and Childwall 1843-1848

Greenall St Helens Deeds Book c1880-1987 (Cheshire Archives)

Greenall Lease Book 1866-1926 (Cheshire Archives)

Liverpool Register of Alehouse Licences 1896-1930 (Liverpool Record Office)

Liverpool Licensing Records 1911-1919 (Liverpool Record Office)

Binns Collection, volume 12 (Liverpool Record Office)

Liverpool Trade Directories 1766-1950

Lancashire Hearth Taxes, Irvine W.F., 1900, Thos. Brakell Ltd. (orig. *Trans. Hist. Soc. Lancashire & Cheshire)*

Prescot Observer and St Helens Advertiser, 1869-1879 (British Library, Boston Spa)

Joseph Jones & Co. Brewers, papers and documents, 1883-1924 (Merseyside Maritime Archives)

'Lancashire', Frank Halliday Cheetham, 1920, Methuen

'A History of the County Palatine and Duchy of Lancaster', Baines E., 1836

'Notes on Childwall', R. Stewart Brown, 1914

'Childwall: A Lancashire Township in the Seventeenth Century', R. Dottie & M. Phil, 1981, *Trans. Hist. Soc. Lancashire & Cheshire Vol. CXXXV*

'Pevsner Architectural Guides: Liverpool', James Sharples, 2004, Yale University Press

'History, Topography and Directory of Mid-Lancashire', P. Mannex, 1855

'Victoris History of the County of Lancaster' pp113-120, W. Farrer & J. Brownbill (eds), 1907

'Ale, Beer and Brewsters in England', Bennett, J.M., 1996, Oxford University Press

'Witches: James I and the English Witch-Hunts', Tracy Borman, 2014, Vintage Books

'The English Inn Past & Present', A.E.Richardson & H.D.Eberlein, 1925, Batsford Ltd.

FURTHER READING AND LOCAL INTEREST

The Old Inns, Taverns and Beer Houses of Woolton, Stuart Rimmer, 2018 (revised 2020), Grosvenor House

Gateacre & Belle Vale: Britain in Old Photographs, Beryl Plent & Mike Chitty, 2009, History Press

The Black Bull, Gateacre: Over 265 Years of Almost Forgotten History, Wilson A.D., 2017